DISCUSSING DEATH
A Guide to Death Education

by

Gretchen C. Mills
Ray Reisler
Alice E. Robinson
Gretchen Vermilye

An ETC Publication
1976

C|P

Library of Congress Cataloging in Publication Data

Main entry under title:

Discussing death.

    Bibliography: p.
    Includes index.
    1. Death.   2. Life.   I. Mills, Gretchen C.,
1947-

BD444.D57   128'.5   75-17885

ISBN 0-88280-026-4
ISBN 0-88280-027-2 pbk.

TABLE OF CONTENTS ✦

Discussing Death
A Guide to Death Education

ACKNOWLEDGEMENTS ✌

We are indebted to many people who have been in direct and indirect assistance in writing this manuscript. We would like to thank the many friends and relatives who have supported our efforts in making this book a reality, and we would like to acknowledge our special gratitude to: Earl Grollman for introducing us to each other; Ward Ghory, for his suggestions in the development of the organizational framework and for his thoughts on "Introducing Death as a Literary Theme;" Giles Hopkins, for his contribution of a significant number of learning opportunities, and also for the abiding good nature and humor he brought to our earlier meetings; Paula Klimek, coordinator of the Human Development Project at South Road School in South Kingston, Rhode Island, for her creative contributions to learning opportunities; Jane R. McCarthy and Deborah Barr, Grandville Heights (Ohio) Public Library, for their assistance in identifying children's books; and Katherine M. Nirote who typed the manuscript in its final form.

INTRODUCTION ✿

Rationale

Why would anyone want to deal with death in the classroom? Everyone's doing it!

Dying, that is.

Startled? Of course. But it can be argued that from the moment of birth every human being is engaged in the process of dying as well as living. Whether or not one subscribes to this outlook, and despite the fact that death is a universal part of living, death is a taboo topic in our society.

Recognizing this taboo, and holding respect for the personal feelings and societal forces which are its foundation, we feel there is a place in the classroom for the introduction and advocacy of death education, and consequently, for making a dent in the stigmas associated with the taboo.

All children, even those younger than six years old, are interested in knowing more about the subject of death, but they are shielded from such exposures in many ways. For example, within the last three or four decades it has become common practice for the sick and elderly to be taken to health care institutions where children are often prohibited, and where death is effectively removed from them. Death occurs less frequently in the home where children can be a part of, and begin to understand, the process of dying.

Children, of course, have other ways of learning about death. Presentations of death in the media constitute a major form of childrens' indirect education; one which strongly influences the impressions of many children. These portrayals of death are often confusing and generally misleading. For example, in American motion pictures death serves primarily as a catalyst for other forms of action, rarely as an emotional reality in itself. Elisabeth Kübler-Ross expands on this point of view in the following quotation:

> The mass media do not ignore death as a part of their programs of entertainment, but they present death in a two-dimensional aspect that tends to make it unreal and devoid of significant emotions. In the two major forms of

television programs, the western and the crime or espionage stories, death is a common thing, but common in the sense that it is treated with disregard . . . This tends to erode the value of life and the reality sense that is essential in coping with major human crises, and further tends to make any important emotions irrelevant and out of place.[1]

Jeffrey Schrank imagines that if dead people could return to life they would "see death hidden from children, the dying isolated from the living, and the schools teaching how to play basketball, solve quadratic equations, and learn who the vice-president in 1898 was. But they would never see the living young learn how to die or even how to live with the certainty of death."[2]

Examples of the ways in which our society denies death have become commonplace in recent literature on death. The results of the 1971 *Psychology Today* questionnaire showed an avoidance of death as a topic of discussion.

So forbidden has death been in our culture that one-third of the respondents could not recall from childhood a single instance of discussion of death within the family circle. In more than one-third of families it was mentioned with discomfort, and in only 30% was death talked about openly.[3]

The *Psychology Today* editors wrote that the 30,000 questionnaire returns established a new record of responses which they believed reveals an urgency to talk about death. But the reluctance of many parents to talk with their children about death shows a marked tendency to protect their young from the pain of loss. Though this is an understandable reaction, most studies in this area conclude that it is more helpful to permit young children to enquire about death, to share memories, observations, and feelings with adults in response to the death of a significant person.

Since this book has been written primarily for teachers, rather than for those who have experience and training as child psychologists, encounter group leaders, etc., stress has been placed

---

[1]Elisabeth Kubler-Ross. *On Death and Dying* (New York: MacMillan Co., 1969), p. 174.
[2]Jeffrey Schrank. *Teaching Human Beings* (Boston: Beacon Press, 1972), p. 175.
[3]Edwin S. Schneidman, "You and Death," *Psychology Today*, Vol. 5, (June, 1971) p. 44.

on the importance of teachers being aware of their students' willingness to discuss their feelings in the classroom. By introducing death in the classroom, children will be given an opportunity to explore many aspects of death on an academic-informational level. The more exposure children have to the subject and the more experience they have in expressing their thoughts and findings, the more comfortable they will become. The focus of this book on informational activities, however, does not preclude emotional involvement and interaction. In fact, it is the sensitive interplay of the informational and emotional approaches (the cognitive and the affective) which will stimulate a deeper understanding and a freer expression of students' thoughts and feelings about death.

Emphasizing the informational-academic approach and simply allowing emotional responses to evolve naturally, in a sense, places a limitation on this work. However, it is a recognized limitation and one which reflects our feelings about the sensitivity required in dealing with death in the classroom. We are hopeful that the integration of the resources and ideas presented in this book will increase the confidence and ability of teachers, students, and parents to regard the subject of death as an important personal and educational topic worthy of open, informed, and sensitive discussion.

This focus upon a single aspect of a child's development should not convey the impression that ideas about death constitute a separate realm in that development. Actually, thoughts of death are intertwined with the total pattern of personality development from the earliest years, influencing and being influenced by all of a child's experiences.

Although this curriculum guide ends at the adolescent level, the person who stays alive psychologically continues to modify his/her orientation toward death throughout life. Certain basic concepts tend to remain firm, but the meaning of death is reexamined as the quality of life changes. This means there is no one true or mature concept of death. Rather, each individual's concept of death undergoes a continuous process of maturing.

Organization of the Guide ✌

This work is based on the belief that the best curricula are created by teachers themselves as they are preparing for their own classes. This book is not accompanied by additional workbooks, printed or audio-visual resources, nor does it lay out step-by-step what teachers should do. The guidelines and resources provided offer a firm foundation which a teacher may use to develop and expand his/her own ideas. This books is not structured as a "death course" although such a course could be composed from the resources presented. Rather, our intention in presenting these activity ideas is to provide teachers of all disciplines the opportunity to integrate activities and discussions about death into on-going classes. Although this guide can be most directly applied in classroom situations, we believe that the wealth of resources and information contained in the book are easily adaptable to other learning environments. The book can be used as a reference, a curriculum guide and a catalyst for any adult interacting with children in the school, home, church, or synagogue.

This curriculum guide includes references to many resources in various media which can be used to open up a wide horizon of innovative learning opportunities for children. The following statements provide the frame of reference upon which this guide was developed:

1. Mental health of children as well as adults depends not upon the denial of tragedy, but upon the frank acknowledgement of it. A well-designed and carefully considered death education program should be made available to all children.

2. As most fears are learned reactions, gaining knowledge about various aspects of death can serve to reduce fears and mis-understandings.

3. It is likely that a child's ability to cope with a particular death may be facilitated if prior discussions of death in general have taken place. Such discussions should introduce the subject gently and in terms the child can understand.

4. Incorporation of death education into the school curricula should not take the form of isolated instruction. Rather, much of the content should be integrated with relevant aspects of the existing curricula.

The guide is separated into four age levels: 5-6 years, 7-9 years, 10-12 years, and 13-18 years. Curriculum concepts and learning opportunities are presented more or less sequentially from the basic to the more difficult. Information preceded by the word *Comment* at the beginning of each age level provides a brief summarization of the general understanding of death by children at that developmental level. We strongly encourage adults to read from the resources on page 83 to more fully learn about the development of a child's conception of death. The format for each learning opportunity is organized in the following manner: Learning Opportunity, Objectives, Activities, and Notes to Teacher. At the end of each age level, complete bibliographical information is given for resources that have been suggested in the learning opportunities.

Although the materials are organized in developmental sequences, learning opportunities at a younger or older level may also be beneficial in meeting the specific needs of individuals. Therefore, the teacher is urged to consider the social and academic maturity of individual students and not feel restricted to the age classifications presented. Since almost all the learning opportunities can be adapted or modified for older or younger students, teachers are encouraged to take advantage of the flexibility of this curriculum guide. For example, in each age level a learning opportunity about life cycles is included which provides an opportunity for expanding an idea if deemed appropriate. In addition to suggesting alternatives and resources for each learning opportunity, the importance of the "Notes to Teacher" section is to stimulate the development of original ideas for new learning opportunities.

Finally, many of the learning opportunities suggest the use of novels, short stories, poems and plays. A literary work has been considered as having relevance for death education if it contains a major or minor theme revealing death as an integral part of the human experience. To help the teacher creatively integrate the numerous literary references, included in the Guide is an outline of various suggested classroom approaches in Appendices A and B. Appendix A is titled "Guidelines From One Teacher's Unit: Introducing Death as a Literary Theme" and Appendix B is titled "Questions To Be Explored Through Fiction." Please refer to these appendices when use of literary works is suggested.

Skill Development 🔄

The development of the following five skills is promoted through all four levels of the curriculum guide. In many learning opportunities, several skills may be developed simultaneously.

1. Development and expression of creativity — Activities are included which enable children to make their own applications of ideas and their own interpretations of content. Activities such as class discussion, dramatization, creative writing and many others are presented.
2. Sensitivity to social and moral values — Learning opportunities reflect a wide range of cultural and social settings and value systems. The goal of the program is not to teach a specific set of values; rather, it is to help children recognize the influence that value systems have on human behavior, and to help them develop their own value systems.
3. Acquisition of knowledge — This skill is promoted through reading, interviewing, and class discussion.
4. Literary understanding and appreciation — The development of this skill is accomplished through study of characterization, mood and theme in a variety of literary works.
5. Study skills — These skills include location of information, organization of information, and use of visual and representational materials, among others.

The Important Role of the Teacher ✌

The rapport a teacher establishes with students is vital to the success of a death education program. Teacher attitudes contribute greatly to the classroom atmosphere. If students feel they can speak freely, the program can be extremely successful.

Consider these points while preparing for student activities:

1. An understanding of death is influenced by the child's ability to comprehend both concrete and abstract concepts.
2. Adults may be called upon to answer questions and offer guidance when they least expect it. As questions arise, the adult must acknowledge them and respond if the child is to benefit from the experience. What teachers say, how they say it, and how they strive to widen the understanding of students is of continual importance. It is important that the child not feel the adult is evading questions. By sensing that the questions do not upset adults, the child will know it is all right to talk about death events.
3. Specific questions asked by a child may not incorporate the aspects of the situation which are of most concern to the child. Teachers must be good listeners and eliciters as well as skillful dispensers of information.
4. All materials should be examined before use and modified as necessary to meet the individual needs of students.
5. Many students will engage in class discussions about death from a religious framework. Recognizing this fact, teachers need to develop learning opportunities which will stimulate examination of various religious customs and beliefs about death. In this way, teachers begin to help students develop an ecumenical understanding of and respect for other people's beliefs.
6. The study of death has the potential for evoking intense emotional reactions. Whether or not this occurs will depend on various unpredictable factors. Therefore, it is important for a teacher to anticipate his/her own responses to these possible occurrences.
7. Facing the reality of death may lead to overwhelming anxiety for a particular student. To cope, the individual may use

avoidance behaviors directed toward the denial of death. If it appears that denial is occurring, the teacher should not attempt to eradicate this coping pattern. With repeated but unpressured opportunities to deal with death in the classroom, the student will increasingly join in activities as he/she becomes more comfortable with his/her own feelings.

8. Although greater emphasis has been placed on the sensitivity and care needed to help children learn about this subject, it is equally important for teachers to explore and begin to confront their own feelings and thoughts about death and death education.

9. The potential for fear and misinterpretation in presenting death education can be looked upon as being analagous to the feelings which were apparent in the earliest days in the development of sex education curricula. Sincere efforts should be made to involve parents, community members (religious leaders, funeral directors, etc.), other teachers, and members of the school administration whenever possible.

LEVEL I: 5-6 Year Olds

LEVEL I: 5-6 Year Olds ✂

Comment

The young child begins with a matter-of-fact orientation to death. He/she believes that death is deliberate and planned; death is not viewed as an inevitable occurrence. Therefore, the young child assumes if he/she is good, death will not occur. Any suggestion that death means personal, total separation is immediately denied. The young child may be prone to misinterpret irrelevant happenings as being intrinsically involved in death. For example, the child may believe that he/she is responsible for the death of a loved one. Because of their natural self-centered focus and limited understanding of cause-effect relationships, young children of this age may not clearly comprehend the finality of death, e.g. squirrels lie dead on the street but identical squirrels run across the yard. Children as well as adults mourn when confronted with the death of a significant person. The fact that a young child does not mourn in a particular manner at a particular time does not mean that he/she does not experience grief and is incapable of mourning.

Concept: Awareness of Feelings ✿

Learning Opportunity:
Feelings

Objectives:
- To explore the abstract realm of feelings.
- To recognize that emotions can be expressed in words.
- To recognize that both happy and sad feelings are a normal part of living.

Activities:
The following illustrated books may be read in small groups and used to stimulate discussion of the children's personal experiences.

Love Is a Special Way of Feeling by Joan Walsh Anglund

What Color is Love? by Joan Walsh Anglund

Feelings by Phoebe and Tris Dunn

How Do I Feel? by Norma Simon

Moods and Emotions, a set of eight full color study prints on 13" x 18" cards, pictures children expressing feelings of love, joy, anger, frustration, compassion, sadness, thoughtfulness, and loneliness. Resource material on the back of each print and the accompanying teacher's manual provide background information for discussion. (The Child's World, P.O. Box 681, Elgin, Ill 60120)

Feelings: What Are You Afraid Of? is a 13 minute film that shows young children talking about their fears and encourages viewers to express fears and seek comfort. (BFA Educational Media, 2211 Michigan Avenue, Santa Monica, Calif. 90404)

How Are You Feeling is an affective program of six filmstrips that show four basic emotions — happiness, sadness, anger and fear. Clown faces help children identify emotions that are then related to human expressions. Response sections call upon the children to identify and match various facial and body expressions. (Bowmar, P.O. Box 3623, Glendale, Calif. 91201).

Two expressive albums recorded by Patty Zeitlin and Marcia Berman may be played again and again as a stimulus for discussion about feelings with young children. *Won't You Be My Friend* explores anger, sadness, fear, growing and changing through songs and rhythm games. *Everybody Cries Sometimes* is another album dealing with these same feelings. The title song assures that even grownups cry and that crying is one way human beings have of recovering from hurts. A copy of the song lyrics is included with each album. (Educational Activities Inc., P.O. Box 392, Freeport, N.Y. 11520)

Notes to Teacher:
The teacher should be alert to the feelings expressed by children in their play. Some chosen play activities may deal directly with death, such as cowboys and Indians, war games, traumatic accidents with dolls and vehicles. The children may be using symbolic play to express death feelings because they may be too painful or because the children lack the language skills to express their feelings with words. Therefore, an adult should not directly question a child about death play. It is possible, however, to ask the child to explain what is happening and express what he/she is actually seeing, e.g., "The car driver smashed the father against the wall." You might want to read *Play Therapy* by Virginia Axline (New York: Ballantine Books, 1969) for further information on childhood play therapy and the adult's role.

Concept: Physical Body Awareness ✺

Learning Opportunity:
  Bodies are Wonderful

Objectives:
  • To identify body parts and their function
  • To identify physical body changes after death occurs.

Activity:
  Elementary games that identify body parts and their functions
can be played. A basic colored illustration of the human body
can be used to discuss the function of: (1) Circulatory system and
heart — the heart keeps everyone alive. Its job is to pump blood
through the body. What color is blood? (2) Lungs — When
people breath through their mouths or noses, they bring air in
through a wind pipe which goes to the lungs. Everybody take a
deep breath and watch what happens to your chest. (3) Bones and
joints — Bones support the body; they help the body stand up, sit
and lie down. (4) Muscles — Muscles are what help the body to
move. They cover the bones and send messages to the brain.
(5) Skin — Skin covers the body and keeps it from being hurt. If
skin is cut, you may bleed a little bit, but the parts inside the
body are too big to come out of a cut.
  Bodies by Barbara Brenner is a photograph book for young
children that explains what human bodies are made of and how
they differ from machines, plants, and each other.
  Death can be explained in terms of the body not working any-
more. E.g., the eyes do not see, the ears cannot hear, the mouth
does not talk, the heart stops beating, the muscles do not move
the arms or legs, the breathing stops and the skin becomes cool.
The children may talk about physical body changes they have
seen in a dead animal.

Concept: Body and Spirit ✿

Learning Opportunity:
   Where Is the Really Me?

Objective:
   • To explore the relationship between the spirit of a person and the physical body.

Activity:
   Where Is the Really Me Game[4]
   Where is the really, really me?
   I'm somewhere, I know, but where can that be?
   I'm not my nose, nor my mouth, nor my eye.
   I'm not my feet, nor my leg, nor my thigh.
   I'm not my hand, nor my arm, nor my hip.
   And I'm not my teeth, nor my tongue, nor my lip.
   I'm sure I'm not my elbow or knee —
   Oh, where am I? Oh where can I be?

Teach the poem to the class so it can be recited together. You may even set the poem to music. After the students are familiar with the words, ask "Where is the part of us that thinks, loves, and feels?" The body may be referred to as the house of the "really me." Point to various body parts asking, "Is this your really me?"

Notes to Teacher:
   When this game has been played several times, you may say the house (body) sometimes gets sick. You may explain that sometimes the body gets so sick that it cannot get well and that doctors are not able to cure all illnesses. However, it is important to stress that this does not happen every time people get sick. The idea that death is directly related to sickness and hospitals should be avoided.

---

[4]Elizabeth Liggett Reed. *Helping Children With the Mystery of Death* (Nashville: Abingdon Press, 1970), p. 33.

Concept: Life Cycles ✿

Learning Opportunity:
Growth and Change

Objective:
• To discuss how growth and change occur in nature.

Activities:
The following books are suggested:

Spring Is A New Beginning and *Morning Is A Little Child* are books by Joan Walsh Anglund which reflect on childhood and the world around us.

Green Eyes by A. Birnbaum shows the changes of the country-side in all four seasons through the eyes of a kitten.

Swamp Spring by Carol and Donald Carrick evokes the wonder of the season's change when winter thaws and plants and animals wake to spring.

The Wonderful Tree by Adelaide Holl presents the precision in the seasonal cycles of growth as a small boy's grandfather reminisces about his childhood.

Hello, Year! is a collection of poetry selected by Leland B. Jacobs on cycles in seasons, weather, and holidays.

The Growing Story by Ruth Krauss is a picture story of the way things in nature grow just as the little boy also grows in his way.

The Wonders of the Seasons by Bertha Morris Parker describes the characteristics and signs of the four seasons in simple text and accurate, detailed pictures.

The Dead Tree by Alvin Tresselt explains how birds, small animals and plants work to return a dead tree to earth.

Students may watch seeds sprout on a wet blotter. The sprouts will die in a few days if they are not planted in soil.

Concept: Cause of Death ✌

Learning Opportunity:
What Makes People Die?

Objectives:
- To understand simple physical reasons for death.
- To reduce perceptions of self-blame for the cause of death.

Notes to Teacher:
There is no specific activity for this concept because the objectives can best be promoted through adult response to the child's spontaneous comments or play activities.

"What makes people die?" asks the young child. It is important to find out why the child has asked this question. The child may feel he/she has caused the death of a significant person. An effective response is to give a simple physical reason for the particular death, explaining that we do not yet know how to cure some diseases or fix some accidents. If the child expresses guilt feelings about the death, adults should help the child develop a new set of non-guilt perceptions about his/her relationship with the deceased by discussing the positive aspects of the relationship. The child needs to be told that the deceased loved him/her, but that the deceased cannot come back to life.

Earl Grollman believes there are three unhealthy explanations of death causation that should be avoided. (1) It is natural to parallel death with sleep, but unless the difference is very carefully explained some children may develop an unhealthy fear of bedtime. Some young children may even believe that Jesus kills people in the night. It is thought that the origin of this belief is founded in the nursery prayer:

Before I lay me down to sleep,
I give the Lord my soul to keep.
And if I die before I wake
I pray the Lord my soul will take.

One can see that this might lead small children to think of sleep in potentially frightening terms. A suggested revision of the bedtime prayer is:

Now I lay me down to sleep,
I pray the Lord Thy child to keep.
Thy love guard me through the night
And wake me in the morning light.

(2) The comparison of death with general sickness might intensify children's fears when they or a loved one becomes ill. (3) Explaining death in relation to God's wanting good people in heaven may cause children to develop fear and resentment toward a God who robbed them of a loved person, and children may feel that because they and others are good, they will also be "taken to heaven."[5]

---

[5]Earl Grollman. *Explaining Death to Children* (Boston: Beacon Press, 1967), pp. 11-12.

Concept: Grief Expression ✧

Learning Opportunity:
Death Makes Me Sad

Objectives:
- To recognize that sad feelings accompanying death are natural.
- To recognize that living goes on despite the grief caused by death.

Activities:
There are several picture books that deal with the concepts related to death for the 5-6 year old child.

Old Dog by Sarah Abbot tells a gentle story of a boy's first encounter with death and of his love for an old dog who will no longer share his life.

Someone Small by Barbara Borak is a gentle story of the growing up of a little girl, her younger sister and a pet bird that dies.

The Dead Bird by Margaret Wise Brown simply describes the physical characteristics of the dead bird and the burial given by the children.

Nana Upstairs, Nana Downstairs by Thomas De Paola is the story of a young boy's relationships with his grandmother and great grandmother. After the great grandmother dies, he learns that death is inevitable.

Scat! by Arnold Dobrin tells of a boy who likes jazz, a form of music grandma calls trash music. When the grandma dies, Scat chooses his own way to say goodbye.

My Grandpa Died Today by Joan Fassler is a story of the love shared by a young boy and his grandfather. When the grandfather dies, David and his family express their sadness. In David's struggle to understand the death, he learns more about life.

When Violet Died by Mildred Kantrowitz describes the children's reactions to a dead parakeet and the funeral preparations and ceremony they have.

The Tenth Good Thing About Barney by Judith Viorst is a story about a cat that died and the little boy who remembers him.

About Dying: An Open Book For Parents and Children Together by Sara Bonnett Stein assists adults in helping and teaching children under eight years of age. Beautiful photographs are included.

After reading and discussing any parts of these books, the children may use crayons, water colors or finger paints to express their feelings. While the children are involved in this art activity, the teacher could talk with them individually about their pictures. Pictures may be displayed on the bulletin board after completion.

Notes to Teacher:

For the most effective results, the teacher should first read and become familiar with the contents of these books. It is not necessary to read the entire book to the children at the first sitting. The pace should be slow and quiet. Pause from time to time to give the children an opportunity to express their feelings and ask questions. Do not push them beyond their emotional capabilities.

Emotional release is natural and highly desirable. Expressions of grief among children should be encouraged as a healthy outlet in minimizing guilt feelings. No one should be ridiculed or admonished for crying. Rather than saying to the child, "There, there, you musn't cry," it is better to say, "I could cry, too." On the other hand, children should not be subjected to emotional blackmail in which they are urged to remain quiet when they want to run and play.

Selected Resources for Level I ✿

Abbot, Sarah. *Old Dog*. New York: Coward, McCann & Geoghegen, 1972.

Anglund, Joan Walsh. *Love Is A Special Way of Feeling*. New York: Harcourt, Brace & World, Inc., 1960.

_____. *Morning Is A Little Child*. New York: Harcourt, Brace & World, Inc., 1969.

_____. *Spring Is A New Beginning*. New York: Harcourt, Brace & World, Inc., 1963.

_____. *What Color Is Love?* New York: Harcourt, Brace & World, Inc., 1966.

Birnbaum, Abe. *Green Eyes*. Wayne, N.J.: Golden Press, 1953.

Borak, Barbara. *Someone Small*. New York: Harper & Row, 1969.

Brenner, Barbara. *Bodies*. New York: E.P. Dutton & Co., 1973.

Brown, Margaret Wise. *The Dead Bird*. Reading, Mass.: Young Scott Books, 1965.

Carrick, Carol and Donald. *Swamp Spring*. New York: MacMillan Co., 1969.

De Paola, Thomas Anthony. *Nana Upstairs, Nana Downstairs*. New York: G.P. Putnam's Sons, 1973.

Dobrin, Arnold. *Scat!* New York: Scholastic, 1971.

Dunn, Phoebe and Tris. *Feelings*. Mankato, Minn.: Creative Education Society, 1971.

Fassler, Joan. *My Grandpa Died Today*. New York: Behavioral Publications, Inc., 1971.

Holl, Adelaide. *The Wonderful Tree*. Wayne, N.J.: Golden Press, 1967.

Jacobs, Leland B., ed. *Hello, Year!* Champaign, Ill.: Garrard Publishing Company, 1972.

Kantrowitz, Mildred. *When Violet Died*. New York: Parents' Magazine Press, 1973.

Krauss, Ruth. *The Growing Story*. New York: Harper & Row, 1947.

Parker, Bertha Morris. *The Wonders of the Seasons*. Wayne, N.J.: Golden Press, 1967.

Simon, Norma. *How Do I Feel?* Chicago: Albert Whitman & Company, 1970.

Stein, Sara Bonnett. *About Dying: An Open Book for Parents and Children Together.* New York: Walk & Co., 1974.

Tresselt, Alvin. *The Dead Tree.* New York: Parents' Magazine Press, 1972.

Viorst, Judith. *The Tenth Good Thing About Barney.* New York: Atheneum, 1971.

LEVEL II: 7-9 Year Olds

LEVEL II: 7-9 Year Olds ✌

Comment

Research indicates that young school children are aware that death is a common finality for all living things and that they associate death with disintegration of the body. Many children up to age ten visualize death in various forms, e.g., as a bogeyman, a skeleton, or a ghost. Other children of this age are able to understand that death does not come in the form of a person and develop a greater understanding of the meaning of physical death from personal experiences. By staying up later at night, young children have more opportunity to see deaths portrayed on television, and they may hear of deaths reported on news programs. To children of this age, death still seems to occur mostly to the old, but they are beginning to sense that it can occur to adults like their parents and possibly even to children like themselves. The question of what happens to the tangible body is of great importance even though adults may stress teachings about the spirit's immortality.

A useful adult resource when dealing with young schoolagers is *Helping Your Child to Understand Death* by Anna W.M. Wolf (New York: Child Study Press, 1973). In this revised edition, the author responds to questions commonly asked by children.

Concept: Life Cycles ♺

Learning Opportunity:
Cycles in Nature

Objective:
- To understand the inevitability of death through the study of cycles in nature.

Activities:
In addition to the books suggested on page 20, *Neighborhood Puddle* by John F. Waters is suggested. Just as there are cycles for the animal life under the water surface, the puddle itself goes through changes caused by the summer weather until finally it disappears in the heat. In *Spring Is Like the Morning* by M. Jean Craig, the sights and sounds of nature in spring after the cold winter illustrate the dependable cycle of time.

Children may keep an almanac or sketchbook of the seasonal changes and the birth and death constantly experienced in nature. Set aside a time each month for a walk in a nature setting to observe and feel these changes. Students may regard their experiences and feelings in a variety of ways — prose, poetry, sketches, water colors, etc. Photographs could also be taken on these outings and mounted on the bulletin board or in a class scrapbook. The class may wish to make a bulletin board that can be added to throughout the year as the seasons change. Students might work in groups or individually to make posters showing nature's cycles.

Students may plant different kinds of seeds and watch them as they grow.

An aquarium may be kept in the classroom where the balance of life and death may be observed.

Notes to Teacher:
Pictures, books and films can stimulate discussions regarding change and growth as seen in nature, e.g., day following night, seasons, larva to butterfly, eggs to tadpoles to frogs. When these cycles in nature are understood, change and growth in people

can be discussed — using the children's experiences. "Where are the babies you used to be?" "Where are the boys and girls your parents used to be?" When the children have developed an attitude of confidence in change, they may discuss what happens to adults as they continue to grow older. "What would happen if old people did not die as more babies are born?"

Learning Opportunity:
After Death, What?

Objective:
• To explore what happens to the physical body after death.

Activities:
In discussing the death of a child's pet or significant person, it would be natural for the teacher to discuss with the class what happens to the physical body. Some children may tell about accompanying their parents to a cemetery and what they saw there — stones with a name to identify each person buried, flowers and bushes. Some children may have participated in a funeral and burial for a neighborhood pet and could share this experience. The burial of a pet provides a real opportunity for children to work things out for themselves and play out their feelings and fears. If a classroom pet dies during the school term, the teacher may suggest such a ceremony be planned and carried out by the children.

Notes to Teacher:
If children press for concrete details about life after death, we can tell them that we do not know what it is like. Grollman believes that the introduction of the traditional idea of heaven may create far more problems than it solves, and that it is healthier for children to share the quest for understanding than for the immediate curiosity to be appeased by fictions.[6] Robert Kastenbaum's article, "The Kingdom Where Nobody Dies" (*Saturday Review/Science*, January, 1973, pp. 33-38.) provides good background information in this area.

---

[6]Grollman, *Explaining Death to Children*, p. 12.

Concept: Grief Expression ✌

Learning Opportunity:
Death Brings Sadness

Objectives:
- To recognize the importance of listening to someone's problem.
- To realize that crying is not a sign of immaturity.
- To understand that living goes on in spite of the grief caused by death.

Activities:
The following books dealing with the expression of grief may be read by and discussed with children 7 to 9 years of age.

The Boy With A Problem by Joan Fassler stresses the importance of listening to one another's problems. Johnny is a boy with a problem that is so big that he does not feel like eating, doing his school work, or playing ball. Many people try to help him by offering all kinds of ideas and suggestions, but it is not until his friend takes time to really listen that Johnny begins to feel better.

Talking About Death by Earl Grollman is a small paperback written as a sharing resource in the adult-child encounter with the helplessness, guilt, loneliness, and fear of death. Grollman emphasizes that the end must always be death, but his words are tender and understanding.

Why Did He Die? by Audrey Harris deals with many typical questions of a young child in a warm, reassuring manner as a mother talks with her son.

John Fitzgerald Kennedy by Patricia Miles Martin is a picture book that represents the life, assassination, and burial of President Kennedy.

Annie and The Old One by Miska Miles is a story about a Navajo girl who cannot imagine her world without her grandmother.

Growing Time by Sandol Warburg tells how a young boy sadly faces the reality of his dog's death and begins to accept the continuity of life through a new puppy.

My Grandson Lew by Charlotte Zolotow tells how six year old Lewis and his mother share their memories of Grandpa and his love.

See *The Day Grandpa Died*, a 12 minute film about a boy's first experience with the death of a loved one. (BFA Educational Media, 2211 Michigan Avenue, Santa Monica, California 90404)

Notes to Teacher:

The books identified for this concept in Level I would also be very appropriate for 7-9 year olds.

Many children of elementary school age who suffer a loss do not show their grief verbally but displace their feelings in other situations. Since school is their natural habitat outside the home, the school situation becomes a main focus for such displacement. Many bereaved children cannot concentrate on their schoolwork, have no desire to play with friends, and hover near their homes. If the security of family life has been suddenly broken, the school-ager may lapse into a long period of apprehensiveness.

It is important for schoolagers to realize that weeping is not a sign of immaturity or weakness. Adults can assist children to understand that sorrow and tears are not for the person who has died but because the departed one will be missed so much. During periods of grief, the adult may provide clay, crayons, or fingerpaints with which the child may express his feelings. The 7-9 years old still has a limited vocabulary for use during stressful situations and may therefore better relieve his/her intense feeling through play.

If a child tells the teacher that a significant person has died, the teacher may ask that the child tell about the happy and not-so-happy times that they had together. Adults can help a child realize that no two people can always have happy times together and that the angry feelings do not lessen the love and strength of the relationship.

Selected Resources for Level II ✌

Craig, M. Jean. *Spring Is Like Morning.* New York: G.P. Putnam's Sons, 1965.

Fassler, Joan. *The Boy With A Problem.* New York: Behavioral Publications, Inc., 1971.

Grollman, Earl A. *Talking About Death.* Boston: Beacon Press, 1970.

Harris, Audrey. *Why Did He Die?* Minneapolis: Lerner Publications Company, 1965.

Martin, Patricia Miles. *John Fitzgerald Kennedy.* New York: G.P. Putnam's Sons, 1964.

Miles, Miska. *Annie and The Old One.* Boston: Little, Brown and Co., 1971.

Warburg, Sandol Stoddard. *Growing Time.* Boston: Houghton Mifflin Co., 1969.

Waters, John F. *Neighborhood Puddle.* New York: Frederick Warne & Company, Inc., 1971.

Zolotow, Charlotte. *My Grandson Lew.* New York: Harper & Row, 1974.

LEVEL III: 10-12 Year Olds

LEVEL III: 10-12 Year Olds ✌

Comment

Most ten year olds have developed sufficiently, both intellectually and emotionally, to understand death as a final and inevitable outcome of life. By age ten the child's distinction between living and non-living is similar to the adult's view. " . . . as the child approaches adolescence he is equipped with most of the intellectual tools necessary to understand both life and death in a logical manner. He now has completed his basic development of concepts of time, space, quantity, and causality."[7] As part of normal intellectual and emotional growth, the schoolager begins to fantasize an alternative to death — a hereafter. Easson believes that in this way schoolagers assure themselves that their newly developed individuality will continue to exist.[8]

---

[7]William M. Easson. *The Dying Child — The Management of the Child or Adolescent Who is Dying* (Springfield, Ill.: Charles C. Thomas, 1970), p. 104.

[8]Ibid., p. 43.

Concept: Life Cycles ↭

Learning Opportunity:
Life-Death Cycles

Objectives:
- To perform experiments which show death and decay as part of the total and natural life cycle in nature.
- To make analogies between plant-animal life cycles and the human life cycle.

Activities:
The following four books all discuss the relationship of living things to each other and their environment: *Understanding Ecology* by Elizabeth T. Billington; *Nature Around the Year* by Henri Leclercq; *A Place in the Sun* by Lois and Louis Darling; and *Ecology — Science of Survival* by Laurence Pringle.

Start two mold cultures and observe the rate of growth with a limited and an unlimited food source.

In science class observe what happens to small animals and plants when they die and decompose. Relate the entire cycle by setting up a small eco-system (possibly in an aquarium) in the classroom. Discuss the relationship between life and death.

Read *Life and Death* by Zim and Bleeker, a small book that discusses the physical facts of and attitudes toward human death in a sensitive manner for this age group. The authors begin by pointing out the range of life spans among plants and animals. The book describes what happens to the human body when it dies, how death is recognized, and burial laws that are followed.

Notes to Teacher:
From a cosmic perspective, death is a reorganization of molecules. Through the miracles of biological and chemical decomposition, the human body quite literally returns to the larger life.

For help in understanding ecology read *Ecology* by Eugene P. Odum (Modern Biology Series, New York: Holt, Rinehart and Winston, 1963).

Concept: Grief Expression ✧

Learning Opportunity:
Grief

Objectives:
- To explore how grief feelings may create self-conflict.
- To identify how characters in novels deal with grief feelings when a significant person or animal dies.

Activities:
Students, individually or in groups, can select a book to share with the whole class.

What Makes Me Feel This Way? by Eda Le Shan discusses various emotions and conflicts, their relationship to physical reactions and other aspects of dealing with one's own feelings. A chapter on death is included in this book.

Death occurs in many family-oriented stories that are written for schoolagers. The most sorrowful of all is perhaps the death of Beth in Louisa Alcott's *Little Women.* Beth takes a tender farewell of life surrounded by her loving family. In *Little Men,* Alcott writes of the death of Meg's husband. There is much that is good in the funeral service and a glimpse of the love that can provide peace for a grieving wife.

Sounder by William Armstrong — A black boy slowly witnesses the death of his father and dog due to sharecropping experiences and the fight for survival. The discovery that things do not die but become part of other things bring the boy new hope.

A Year in the Life of Rosie Bernard by Barbara Brenner — After her mother's death, Rosie spends a year living with relatives. On one of her actor father's visits, he brings a woman friend.

Uncle Mike's Boy by Jerome Brooks — Eleven year old Pudge and his sister supported one another after their parents' divorce.

After Sharon's accidental death, Pudge felt desolate and alone, but through his uncle's attention he gained self-confidence.

The Big Wave by Pearl Buck — After Jiya's tragic loss of his parents in a great tidal wave, his foster-father, with wisdom and gentleness, helps Jiya recover from his shock, accept death, and live again with a heart free of bitterness.

Ellen Grae by Vera and Bill Cleaver — Ellen Grae had a vivid imagination but she did not fabricate the strange secret told to her by Ira, a simple man who lived by the river. Since she knew the awful thing that happened in the swamp years ago was true she had to make a decision between her affection for Ira and her sense of what was right.

Grover by Vera and Bill Cleaver — Eleven year old Grover knew his mother was dying with an illness. When she killed herself with a gun, everyone said it was an accident, but Grover knew this was not true. His confusion thrashes out in bursts of rage and finds no comfort from his father.

Anne and the Sand Dobbies by John Coburn is eleven year old Danny's story about his dog that was killed and his sister who died. Through the help of an adult friend and the sand dobbies, Danny reaches his own understanding of what it means to die.

Thank You, Jackie Robinson by Barbara Cohen — The only person who shared Sam's enthusiasm for the Dodgers was Davey, the elderly black cook who worked for Sam's widowed mother. Davy took Sam to many baseball games until he had a heart attack. When Davey died, Sam struggled to understand.

Tistou of the Green Thumbs by Maurice Druon — A young child discovers he has a green thumb which he uses to place flowers in prisons, slums, zoos, and guns. When his friend, the gardner, dies, the child discovers that his flowers will not bring back the friend.

The Day They Gave Babies Away by Dale Eunson — In the summer of 1868 Robert Eunson died of diptheria. Mamie died of fever in December. After the funeral, twelve year old Bob found homes for his brothers and sisters as his mother had requested.

The River by Rumer Godden — As a white girl growing up in India, Harriet first encountered death through the Buddhist rituals and then with a dead guinea pig. But when her brother died suddenly from a cobra bite, Harriet's struggle to understand becomes very personal.

The Magic Moth by Virginia Lee — When ten year old Maryanne dies after a long illness, six year old Mark-O and the rest of the family become a little wiser about death.

Home From Far by Jean Little — After Jenny's twin brother was killed in an auto accident, her parents decide to help the family adjust to a new life.

In *Jonathan* by Margaret Lovett, a fourteen year old boy assumes responsibility for five orphaned children in nineteenth century England. The story tells of the life of the poor in potteries, mines, and mills where the death of children was expected.

In *The Mulberry Music* by Doris Orgel, an eleven year old girl slowly realizes that her grandmother is not just sick, but is dying. As Libby defies parents, hospital rules, and locked doors in her search for Grandmother, she gains an understanding of how love survives.

The House Without a Christmas Tree by Gail Rock — In 1946, ten year old Addie tried to understand her father's objection to having a Christmas tree. In the process she learned more about her dead mother and grief responses.

The Thanksgiving Treasure by Gail Rock — On Thanksgiving in 1947, Addie set out to make friends with a family enemy. Old man Reinquist and Addie develop an unusual friendship. When the old man dies, Addie must deal with confusing feelings she has never known before.

Shadow of a Bull by Maia Rodman — A boy is expected to follow in his father's footsteps and become a fighter of bulls and a killer of death. This book examines the boy's predicament and eventual decision to chose another career.

The Truth About Mary Rose by Marilyn Sacks tells how a young girl named after an aunt who died in a fire learns more about her aunt's life.

A Taste of Blackberries by Doris Buchanan Smith — Jamie's exuberance and a harmless prank end in sudden tragedy. The boy narrator of this story deals with his grief and the feeling of guilt that he might have saved his friend.

Away Is So Far by Tony Talbot — A young boy whose mother has died is left to struggle with his own feelings while his father is locked inside his own grief.

J.T. by Jane Wagner — This is a story of a nine year old inner city child who develops a beautiful relationship with a stray cat that, in time, is killed by a car.

The Golden Treasury of Myths and Legends by Anne T. White From these greek, Roman, and Norse myths adapted for children, stories may be selected to compare the manner of grief expression with modern stories.

Charlotte's Web by E.B. White — This is a story of the friendship between Wilbur, a pig, and Charlotte, a large grey spider. By a clever plan of her own thinking, Charlotte saves Wilbur from the death he feared. But Wilbur's joy is not complete because of Charlotte's inevitable autumn death.

The Bird's Christmas Carol by Kate Douglas Wiggin — This is a classic story about ten year old Carol Bird, a young invalid, who shares her last family Christmas.

Walking Away by Elizabeth Winthrop — Every summer was spent joyously at her grandparents' farm and Emily never thought of time passing. But this summer her best friend came to visit and life would never be the same.

Selected Resources for Level III ⟳

Alcott, Louisa May. *Little Men*. Originally published, 1871.
_____. *Little Women*. Originally published, 1869.
Armstrong, William H. *Sounder*. New York: Harper & Row, 1969.
Billington, Elizabeth T. *Understanding Ecology*. New York: Frederick Warne & Co., Inc., 1968.
Brenner, Barbara. *A Year in the Life of Rosie Bernard*. New York: Harper & Row, 1971.
Brooks, Jerome. *Uncle Mike's Boy*. New York: Harper & Row, 1973.
Buck, Pearl. *The Big Wave*. New York: John Day, 1952.
Cleaver, Vera and Bill. *Ellen Grae*. Philadelphia: J.B. Lippincott Co., 1967.
_____. *Grover*. Philadelphia: J.B. Lippincott Co., 1970.
Coburn, John B. *Anne and the Sand Dobbies*. New York: Seabury Press, 1964.
Cohen, Barbara. *Thank You, Jackie Robinson*. New York: Lothrop, Lee & Shepard Co., 1974.
Darling, Lois and Louis. *A Place in the Sun*. New York: William Morrow & Co., 1968.
Druon, Maurice. *Tistou of the Green Thumbs*. New York: Scribner, 1958.
Eunson, Dale. *The Day They Gave Babies Away*. New York: Farrar, Straus & Giroux, 1946.
Godden, Rumer. *The River*. Boston: Little, Brown & Co., 1946.
Leclercq, Henri. *Nature Around the Year*. Wayne, N.J.: Golden Press, 1972.
Lee, Virginia. *The Magic Moth*. New York: Seabury Press, 1972.
Le Shan, Eda. *What Makes Me Feel This Way?* New York: MacMillan Co., 1972.
Little, Jean. *Home From Far*. Boston: Little, Brown & Co., 1965.
Lovett, Margaret. *Jonathan*. New York: E.P. Dutton, 1972.
Orgell, Doris. *The Mulberry Music*. New York: Harper & Row, 1971.
Pringle, Laurence. *Ecology — Science of Survival*. New York: MacMillan Co., 1971.

Rock, Gail. *The House Without a Christmas Tree*. New York: A.A. Knopf, 1974.

_____ . *The Thanksgiving Treasure*. New York: A.A. Kopf, 1974.

Rodman, Maia. *Shadow of a Bull*. New York: Atheneum, 1964.

Sacks, Marilyn. *The Truth About Mary Rose*. Garden City, N.Y.: Doubleday & Co., 1973.

Smith, Doris Buchanan. *A Taste of Blackberries*. New York: Thomas Y. Crowell Co., Inc., 1973.

Talbot, Toby. *Away Is So Far*. New York: Scholastic, 1974.

Wagner, Jane. *J.T.* New York: Van Nostrand Reinhold Co., 1969.

White, Anne Terry. *The Golden Treasury of Myths and Legends*. New York: Golden Press, 1959.

White, E.B. *Charlotte's Web*. New York: Harper & Row, 1952.

Wiggin, Kate Douglas. *The Bird's Christmas Carol*. Boston: Houghton, Mifflin, 1941.

Winthrop, Elizabeth. *Walking Away*. New York: Harper & Row, 1973.

Zim, Herbert S. and Bleeker, Sonia. *Life and Death*. New York: William Morrow & Co., 1970.

LEVEL IV: 13-18 Year Olds

LEVEL IV: 13-18 Year Olds

Comment ✌

The teenager has the mental and emotional capacity to sense the personal depth of meaning in death.

> Sooner or later the adolescent is likely to turn his new intellectual resources to the subject of death. Previously he had been led to believe certain propositions about "life after death" — now he may be inclined to examine these propositions critically. Furthermore, it is not enough to acknowledge the bare reality of death. Somehow, this reality must become integrated into his total view of life. As the adolescent begins to form his own purpose and make his own decisions he becomes aware that all his hopes, expectations, ambitions, require time for their actualization. The adolescent stands here, at a certain point in time. Off in the distance, on the other side of time, stands death. This new self that he is developing and these new purposes that are emerging confront a natural enemy in death.[9]

The teenager's understanding of the implications of personal death can lead to a fuller appreciation of life, but he/she may have difficulty applying fears about death in a positive way. Fears and hesitations which mark initial efforts to explore the subject of death with 13 to 18 year old students tend to diminish as the opportunity to share their feelings brings emotional relief and excitement for learning. Sharing feelings, getting to know one another, and making decisions on goals and methods pertaining to class projects are basic activities for students of this highly eruptive and emotional age. The teacher must be a facilitator and a catalyst first and a subject matter specialist second. Classroom and community activities should be constructed around the problems of the

---

[9]Earl Grollman, *Explaining Death to Children* (Boston: Beacon Press, 1967), pp. 104-105.

students and the social issues of the times. Death education learning opportunities can meet these needs in novel and provocative ways.

Since many of the learning activities in Part IV involve the use of literature — poems, plays, novels, biographies, please refer to the appendices for further teacher suggestions. Appendix A is "Guidelines from One Teacher's Unit: Introducing Death as a Literary Theme." Appendix B is "Questions to be Explored through Fiction."

Concept: Life Cycles ✿

Learning Opportunity:
Mathematics of Life and Death

Objectives:
- To use birth and death statistics and their graphic representations to compare human life cycles in different times and geographical locations.
- To become familiar with the use of mathematics in studying birth and death.

Activity:
Using reference materials from the library (almanacs, current periodicals, encyclopedias, etc.) look up vital statistics on birth and death for various countries having different geographical locations and different socio-economic standards. With a series of graphs, represent the differences from country to country. Discuss possible reasons for these differences. Also investigate the birth and death statistics for the United States at several periods in history. Discuss factors which have influenced the trends in these statistics. What are the implications of the decreasing death rate?

Notes to Teacher:
This exercise would be a good introduction to discussing the population explosion and the controversy surrounding the trends in population growth. Teachers may want to refer to the *Limits to Growth* by Donella Meadows, et. al. (Washington, D.C.: Potomac Books, Inc., 1972), and the Malthusian theory of population growth. If you are not a math whiz, this would be a good opportunity to do some team teaching.

This activity could be adopted in fifth and sixth grades as a combined social science/math unit. You could discuss the differing life styles of the countries which show extreme, as well as moderate graph results in light of climate, location, economics, social organization, etc.

Learning Opportunity:
Growth and Death in Nature

Objectives:
- To discuss death from a biological perspective.
- To make analogies betwen plant-animal life cycles and the human life cycle.

Activities:
Investigate the ability of a group of cells to survive apart from the total organism by:

—studying the ability of the planaria (small ciliated worm) to reproduce itself from only a few body cells, and/or
—creating roots which live and grow apart from the whole plant.

In science class, place a few fruit flies in an enclosed container with a food source. Observe how fast the fruit flies multiply until the food source is eliminated. This activity may stimulate a discussion on population explosion and world food needs.

Show *To Say Goodbye*, a documentary film which deals with the natural balance of the eco-system and how man interferes with it. (Films Inc. Distribution Center, 733 Greenbay Road, Urtmette, Illinois 60091) Class discussion may follow the film showing.

Learning Opportunity:
Death and Life Processes

Objective:
- To investigate how one body organ or system changes during the dying process and àt death.

Activity:
Pick one of the major systems of the body (circulatory, respiratory, etc.) or a major organ of the body (liver, kidney, etc.) and study how it functions and how it ceases to function due to various causes of death (poison, pollution, drugs, natural cause).

If in the normal teaching of your class you are dealing with the life functions of various organs and systems, it may be valuable to explore what happens to those organs and systems during the dying process and at death. Consider differences due to death by poison, pollution, drugs, natural causes, etc.

Learning Opportunity
Living or Dying?

Objective:

- To explore questions about the processes of living and dying.

Activity.
Consider and discuss the following questions:

- Imagine that, starting today, death ceases to exist at any biological level. What are the implications?

- From our embryonic life onward, certain cells in our systems are dying. An observable example is the cells of our skin. By dying they perform a life sustaining function for our total organism. This process extends to other organs as we mature, and the process of deterioration begins at about age 18. Are we living or dying? Is the process of living and dying in our bodies a microcosmic representation of all life?

- Rather than allow the process of evolution to be directed by natural selectivity or calamity, will humans seek to limit and control their own evolution through selective creation and selective destruction of human life? What are the implications?

Notes to Teacher:
A thought: Can we continue to eliminate death from the facts of life and expect humanity to survive?

Each of the above topics may be used for subjects of written theme assignments and/or for class discussion.

You may enjoy reading the following reference which may be shared with the class:

Jones, Claiborne S. "In the Midst of Life," in *Explaining Death to Children*, ed. Earl A. Grollman (Boston: Beacon Press, 1970).

Learning Opportunity:
Youth

Objectives:
- To heighten awareness of the premium value attached to being young which causes aging to seem more abhorrent.
- To survey the attitudes toward youth and aging that are presented by the media.

Activities:
Collect evidence of the marketable value of youthfulness.
- Make a bulletin board or collage of advertisements, headlines, stories, etc. from magazines and newspapers.
- Collect references on the fear and/or disdain of aging from conversation, the media, jokes, etc.

Ask people who have lost their jobs in middle age to speak to the class about the frustrations and discouragement while searching for reemployment. Or ask an employment counsellor for such information.

Through class discussion and/or small group projects develop a survey form that each student can use while watching television programs, cartoons, and commercials. The survey form should include items that will note the glorification of youth and the stigma associated with aging. After using the survey form for a given time period (two days to two weeks), tabulate and discuss the results. Class representatives might be able to appear on the local television or radio station's community show to present your findings.

The class might invite a representative from the local television station to discuss television's role in relaying healthy attitudes toward aging.

Read "The Tree of Life" by Harvey Swados. In this short story an aging man, by his own acceptance of life and death, inspires his nephew who is terrified of growing old.

Notes to Teacher:
The class may eventually be able to identify their feelings about being young and discuss them. Perhaps they will learn that the fear of aging is conditioned into us, and begin to explore a more positive attitude toward the inevitability of time.

You might refer to "The Soul and Death" by Carl Jung, Chapter 1 in *The Meaning of Death* edited by Herman Feifel (New York: McGraw-Hill, 1959).

Learning Opportunity
If I Had It To Do Over Again

Objectives:
• To identify with the process of aging and its reality.
• To evaluate student readiness or reluctance to approach the the subject of aging and dying.

Activity:
A dialogue, fantasy, and role play:
1) What age would you like to be if you could?
2) Imagine that you are that age. What is your life like now? Are you looking forward to being another age? What age? Why? Continue until the students begin to resist getting older.
3) At what stage does aging become a worry? When do we stop aspiring to be older? Why? When might we begin to say, "If only I had it to do over again . . ."?
4) Return to your own age. If you had it to do over again now, what would you do differently?
5) Imagine the impact of having someone else ask you that question when you are seventy years old. Imagine that you are seventy years old. What would you like to have accomplished? What will you want your life to be like at that age?
6) Have the class or an individual role play life at age seventy. Set the scene with a few aches, perhaps dim vision, etc. Ask such questions as: Are you married? How many children

and grandchildren do you have? Are you living alone? Can you support yourself? What had you hoped to accomplish? What prevented you from reaching your goals if you fell short? Who helped/hindered you? How do you feel about being aged? Why?

Notes to Teacher:
Aging in our society is equated with uselessness, aloneness, pitifulness, and imminent death. The aged are frequently outcasts. Perhaps, if youth can consider the cruel reality of these facts and ponder the reasons for them, attitudes may be changed.

Learning Opportunity:
Silver Threads

Objectives:
- To reflect on problems involved in being an elderly person in the community.
- To reflect on one's own values on aging.

Activities:
Visit with an elderly person in that person's home or in a nursing home. (Small student groups could go to a nursing home together.) Share your experiences through class discussion or express your thoughts through creative writing, art, or song.

Possible related activities:
- Make the visits available once a week for anyone who wishes to go.
- Keep a diary of personal impressions, reactions, activities, thoughts.
- Make a scrapbook or collage of photographs taken on your visits. The collection of photographs could be given to the elderly person.
- Tape record a conversation with an elderly person and share it with the class.

The following films may be used to stimulate class discussion:
  Aging (30 min., color) Two elderly Jewish men discuss their lives, loneliness, and feelings toward youth as they play cards. (Indiana Univ. A.V. Center, Bloomington, Indiana 47401)

The Art of Age (27 min., color) Four retired people, each with a healthy approach to living, talk about their lives. They provide insight into the minds of older people and show varied constructive ways to use retirement. (ACI Films, 35 W. 45th Street, New York, N.Y. 10036)

Mr. Story (27 min., color) This is a portrait of a self-sufficient 87 year old man, whose observations on morals, marriage, work, women's liberation, and life as an old person are profound and entertaining. (Thacher/Halleck Productions, 33 Second Ave., New York, N.Y. (10003)

Nell and Fred (29 min., b & w) A true story of two old people faced with the decision of whether to move into senior-citizen housing or live alone. (McGraw-Hill Films, 1221 Ave. of the Americas, New York, N.Y. 10020)

Peege (28 min., color) A young man visiting his grandmother is able to communicate through sharing of early memories and by using human touch to express closeness. (Phoenix Films, 470 Park Ave. So., New York, N.Y. 10016)

The Rights of Age (28 min., b & w) An examination of the kinds of social services needed by the elderly, focusing on the case of a lonely widow. (International Film Bureau, 332 S. Michigan Ave., Chicago, Ill. 60604)

To Be Growing Older (13 min., color) Comments from old people are alternated with young people's views of old age. (Billy Budd Films, 235 E. 57th St., New York, N.Y. 10022)

Tomorrow Again (16 min., b & w) A few minutes in the life of a lonely old woman are shown. (Pyramid Films, P.O. Box 1048, Santa Monica, Cal. 90406)

When Parents Grow Old (15 min., color) This edited version of the movie *I Never Sang for My Father* explores one's responsibility to aging parents. ("Searching for Values" series, Learning Corp. of America, Film Rental Library, 50-30 Northern Blvd., Long Island City, N.Y. 11101

To the Teacher:
It is hoped that talking with elderly persons will help erase some of the stigma against aging. Some students respond with enthusiasm and increased participation to this project. Others seem to be thoroughly disinterested, perhaps reflecting their wish to ignore the reality of the inevitability of their own futures. This activity can be adapted for any age group.

Additional resources to be used for this experience include:

Malveaux, Marie. *Report of the Youth-Aging Project*, 1972. Send to: Catholic Committee for Aging, Rm. 202, 50 Oak Street, San Francisco, California 94102 ($2.00).

Townsend, Claire. *Old Age: The Last Segregation.* New York: Grossman Publishers, 1971.

Welty, Eudora. "A Visit of Charity," in *Selected Stories of Eudora Welty.* New York: Modern Library, 1954.

Concept: Death Causes ✿

Learning Opportunity:
Cancer and Uncontrolled Growth

Objectives:
- To understand cancer as a disease characterized by uncontrolled growth.
- To explore implications of cancer in the broader understanding of the term.

Activities:
Do research projects on cancer. A good resource is "King Cancer" by Philip Nobile in *Esquire* (June, 1973), pp. 103-111. Students may wish to interview local physicians and other medical professionals. These people might be asked to talk with the class.

Consider also the implications of the dynamics of cancer for the world at large. Cancer is, by definition, a cell or cells that do not have a natural mechanism of death. That is, cells growing unchecked until they become destructive. Uncontrolled growth (life) brings death to a human being. What are the implications of this understanding of cancer for a greater society which has no mechanism to deal with dying, death, and over-population?

Learning Opportunity:
Suicide and You

Objectives:
- To explore feelings about self-destruction.
- To study suicide as a mode of death.

Activities:
When reading and discussing the following books, consider why the character committed suicide and whether other characters could or should have stopped the suicide.

Craig and Joan: Two Lives for Peace by Eliot Asinof is a true report of a dual teenage suicide.

A Clean, Well-Lighted Place by Ernest Hemingway is a short story that relates people's feelings about an old man who attempted suicide.

A Blues I Can Whistle by A.E. Johnson — The journal of an 18 year old boy reveals the web of emotions that led to his suicide attempt.

The Heart Is a Lonely Hunter by Carson McCullers — John Singer, a deaf mute who is forced to listen and not "talk" becomes the recipient of the confidences of several town residents. John's only friend, another deaf mute, has been committed to an asylum.

A Figure of Speech by Norma F. Mazer — Thirteen year old Jenny learns that her parents plan to move Grandpa into an old folk's home and events lead to tragedy as Grandpa attempts to salvage his dignity.

The Death of a Salesman by Arthur Miller ends with the suicide of an aging family member.

In A Darkness by James A. Wechsler is a personal memoir about the author's son who killed himself at age 26 after years of psychotherapy.

"The Man in the Middle" by Loudon Wainwright (*Life*, July 21, 1972 issue) is the true story of a black assistant principal in Flint, Michigan. In the midst of the high school's racial strife, he chose to commit suicide. Another account of this situation is entitled "Tragedy at Beecher High" by Vern E. Smith in *Ebony*, October, 1972.

Study the system for classifying modes of death proposed by Edwin Shneidman. His three categories — intentioned, unintentioned, and subintentioned — are presented in "The Enemy" in *Psychology Today* (August, 1970), pp. 37-41.

Take an opinion poll of the student body to see how many have considered suicide, no matter how lightly. Also ask whether an individual should be allowed to commit suicide if he/she so desires.

Popular music referring to suicide, statistics regarding suicides, and newspaper articles may be used to stimulate class discussion. For example, most American newspapers reported about Christine Chubbuck's suicide committed on a morning television news show August 2, 1974. Important questions to consider during discussion include: Who owns one's body? Is there a right to suicide? What happens with the family and friends of people who commit suicide?

Write a short story on the suicide of an imaginary friend. Explore the reasons for the friend's death and include your own reactions to the suicide.

Compile a list of community resources (mental health clinics, crisis centers, hospitals, hot lines, etc.) for referral in assisting each other with various types of problems including suicide.

Talk with psychologists or staff at a suicide prevention center to answer questions such as: Why do some teenagers commit suicide? Are persons who threaten suicide really serious? What can I do if a friend indicates he/she might commit suicide? What are the motivations for committing suicide? How can teenagers meaningfully help each other with problems, especially if a friend seems to be suicidal?

Interview emergency room personnel about the treatment of attempted suicides. Talk with policemen and women about their training and attitudes about suicide.

Publications on suicide are available from the Center for Studies of Suicide Prevention, National Institute of Mental Health, 5600 Fishers Lane, Rockville, Md., 20852. Students should write first for the list of publications and then order those of interest.

Notes to Teacher:
According to *The New York Times*, April 16, 1973, suicide is the second leading cause of death amont 15-24 year olds. Students want to know about suicide and especially how to help a friend who is suicidal.

You may want to look at these resource books:
Alexander, I.E., and Norman L. Faberow, "Suicide and Death," in *The Meaning of Death*, ed. by Herman Feifel. New York: McGraw-Hill, 1959.
Cain, Albert, ed. *Survivors of Suicide*. Springfield, Ill.: C.C. Thomas, 1972.
Durkiteim, Emile. *Suicide*. New York: Free Press, 1951.

Grollman, Earl. *Suicide: Prevention, Intervention, Postvention.* Boston: Beacon Press, 1971.

Jacobs, Jerry. *Adolescent Suicide.* New York: Wiley-Interscience, 1971.

Meerloo, Joost A. *Suicide and Mass Suicide.* New York: E.P. Dutton, 1968.

Shneidman, Edwin S., ed. *On the Nature of Suicide.* San Francisco: Jossey-Bass, 1969.

Concept: Grief Expression ✿

Learning Opportunity:
To Say Goodbye

Objective:
- To recognize the importance of sharing one's feelings about separations with the person(s) involved.

Activity:
In a classroom discussion share a time when you or someone close to you moved/went away. Tell what this meant to you. Then, to finish the unfinished goodbyes, send a telegram orally saying "I want you to know . . . ," "I never told you . . . ," to the person(s) you are talking about. Open the discussion to the whole group using the same format with each person getting five minutes. Or divide the group into triads. One minute should be used to send the telegram.[10]

Notes to Teacher:
Saying goodbye evokes many feelings and is difficult for most people. We are living in a time of rapid change and people are continually moving in and out of our lives. We have not been taught the importance of saying goodbye to people who are important to us. Thus, we carry around unfinished business in many relationships. When the time comes that we have to face death, we bring to it the feelings of many unfinished goodbyes.

A follow-up assignment could be a paper or an oral presentation for the next day on what the student felt or did not feel about the experience. Students should be told that they have the freedom to disclose only what they are ready to disclose.

Learning Opportunity:
How Do We Adjust To Death?

---

[10]Adapted from *Values Clarification* by Sidney B. Simon, et. al. (New York: Hart, 1972).

Objective:
- To explore coping mechanisms used to deal with grief.

Activity:
Compare the stages of adjustment to dying with some that we use in lesser crises. What are some experiences that the class can recall or imagine that might compare to the following which are used in coping with dying?
1) Denial, isolation, and repression
2) Anger
3) Bargaining
4) Depression
5) Acceptance

Notes to Teacher:
Perhaps some of the following examples would be useful in helping the students relate to these emotions.
1) The experience of being deprived forever of something that one wanted badly.
2) Moving away from a loved home and friends forever.
3) A broken love affair.
4) Losing a game because of bad luck.

Elisabeth Kübler-Ross describes these mechanisms in *On Death and Dying* (New York: MacMillan Company, 1969).
Vanderlyn R. Pine, in chapter 6, "Dying, Death and Social Behavior," of *Anticipatory Grief* (ed. Arthur C. Carr, et al. New York: Columbia University Press, 1974.) suggests that grief is a separate process which has its own stages of development. These bear a similarity to the stages of adjustment to dying suggested by Elisabeth Kübler-Ross. These are:

1) Disbelief
2) Questioning
3) Anger
4) Resignation, Dismay, Dispair
5) Resolution

Learning Opportunity:
To Console

Objectives:
- To explore the feelings of empathy and sympathy.
- To convey something personal to another person.

Activities:
Through the use of roleplay, act out situations in which a teenager is trying to console another person. Situations which may be written about by the teacher or students might include:
- Your best friend is upset about a broken love affair.
- Your best friend just broke his leg before he was to compete in the state track meet.
- You are the one who must tell your eight year old sister the family pet has been killed.
- Your best friend's father died unexpectedly of a heart attack.
- Your best friend's twin was killed in a motorcycle accident.

Write a note of condolence to your friend for one of the above situations or make up a situation of your own. Also try writing a condolence note to an older person. Exchange the letters within the class, and each student, imagining that he/she is the bereaved person, will write a reply.

Notes to Teacher:
Empathy and sympathy are difficult to help someone learn. It is not unusual for students to feel awkward trying to console someone. If students are reluctant to roleplay before the entire class, divide into small groups. Since you cannot be present in each group, the students will need to assume more responsibility in analyzing each roleplay.

You might find these resources helpful:

Bereavement and the Process of Mourning (a $15 Cassette) from The Center for Death Education and Research, 1167 Social Sciences Building, Univ. of Minnesota, Minneapolis, Minn., 55455.

Parkes, Colin Murray. *Beareavement/Studies of Grief in Adult Life*. New York: International Universities Press, 1972.

Schoeberg, Bernard, et. al. *Loss and Grief: Psychological Management in Medical Practice*. New York: Columbia University Press, 1970.

Learning Opportunity:
Death and Grief in Literature

Objectives:
- To analyze death themes in literature.
- To explore differences in individual responses to grief through the study of literary works.

Activities:
Read from the following list of books and plays which contain death themes.

Short Stories:

"My Old Man" by Ernest Hemingway — Joe grieves after seeing his jockey father killed in a race and learning that his father had been corrupt.

"The Dead" by James Joyce — A man shares his wife's grief over the death of her admirer many years ago.

"A Painful Case" by James Joyce — A lonely man reflects upon his state of life and brief affair with a woman after reading of her death in the newspaper.

"The Sisters" by James Joyce — A boy listens to adults talk about his dead friend, a priest, after seeing his prepared corpse.

"Tell Me a Riddle" by Tillie Olsen — The adult children observe the deep cleavage between their aging parents. A terminal illness brings the wife to no forgiveness, but prior to her death the surviving husband is able to regain feelings of tenderness and to lessen his feelings of guilt.

"From Mother . . . With Love" by Zoa Sherburne — The adolescent, aware of her mother's imminent death, is able to get much of the grief work over before the actual death.

"My Uncle's Death" by John Updike — An adolescent's experience with death and funerals gives him new perceptions of family roles.

Novels:

A Death in the Family by James Agee — A sensitive account of how a family and particularly a six year old boy respond to the death of the father.

The Blanket Word by Honor Arundel — Faced with the ugliness of her mother's death and the farce of going through the funeral, nineteen year old Jan is convinced she wants no part of family life. However, after returning to her normal college life, she attempts to balance her sense of self with the needs of others.

Dream of the Blue Heron by Victor Barnouw — A young Chippewa Indian boy growing up at the turn of the century is caught in the conflict between his traditional forest-dwelling grandparents and his father who brings Wabus into the modern world. The boy's struggle to find his own way is changed after his grandfather is accidentally killed in a fight by Wabus's father. An authentic portrayal of Chippewa ceremonies, including the funeral, is given. (Jr. High)

Reunion in December by Carole Bolton — The tragedy of her father's unexpected death had a shattering effect upon fourteen year old Eileen, her brother and mother. Seventeen months later when the family gathers for a reunion, Eileen comes to grips with herself as she learns that she will have to accept a new father. (Jr. High)

Wuthering Heights by Emily Bronte — In this stormy novel set on the wild moorlands of England, the characters' fierce passions go unrestrained.

The Good Earth by Pearl Buck — This novel tells of the lives and deaths in a Chinese peasant family.

Where the Lilies Bloom by Vera and Bill Cleaver — After the death of both her parents, a fourteen year old Appalachian girl leads her three siblings in their struggle to survive the long, bitter winter. (Jr. High)

Red Badge of Courage by Stephen Crane — A Civil War recruit matures with the life-death, hope-despair experiences he encounters.

Wild in the World by John Donovan — John, the last surviving member of the Gridley family, tried to do all the jobs his family had done. This mountain youth had a hard life until a wild animal became his friend. Finally John dies in a strange way. (Jr. High)

Incident at Hawk's Hill by Allan W. Eckert — Six year old Ben ran away from his family's farm and survived the summer in the wilds, cared for by a badger who lost her litter. Ben is eventually found but his animal is cruelly shot. (Jr. High)

Another Part of the House by Winston M. Estes — This novel of Texas family life in the Depression is told through the eyes of ten year old Larry. After the death of his sixteen year old brother, Larry gains new understanding about the affirmation of life through the guidance of his parents.

A Place of Her Own by Ann Mari Falk — After her parents were drowned, 15 year old Stina had to adjust to a new way of life in Stockholm with her married sister's family.

As I Lay Dying by William Faulkner — Enclosing their dead mother in a home-made coffin, five children load her on a wagon and, accompanied by the dazed father, travel for several days across a rain-swept country to bury her with her folks. Flooding rivers, a decaying corpse, buzzards and a demented small boy intrude upon the reader's senses.

The Autobiography of Miss Jane Pittman by Ernest J. Gaines This is a novel in the guise of taperecorded recollections of a black woman who has lived through the deaths of many beloved persons in her years from slavehood to her present age of 110.

The Snow Goose by Paul Gallico — This is a story of a lonely man who cared for wild things and a girl who learned to see beyond his ugly appearance. The warmth of her feelings became known after his death helping fellow countrymen in war.

The Summer After the Funeral by Jane Gardam — Following the death of their father, the three Pierce children stay with various acquaintances. Sixteen year old Athene's summer is filled with disturbing people and experiences.

Our Mother's House by Julian Gloag — After the death of their mother, thirteen year old Elsa and the six younger children bury her in the garden. To protect themselves from an orphanage, they pretend she is ill, and their struggle to keep this secret brings dissention among them.

Cross-Fire: A Vietnam Novel by Gail Graham — An American soldier lost from his platoon finds four enemy children, the only survivors of a village air raid. Together they begin the doomed struggle to reach help. (Jr. High)

The Friends by Rosa Guy — Fourteen year old Phyllisia eventually recognizes that her own pride, rather than her mother's death and tyrannical behavior, created the gulf between herself and her devoted friend. (Jr. High)

Mythology by Edith Hamilton — This retelling of Greek, Roman and Norse myths in modern prose will enable young persons to compare grief expression of mythological characters with characters in modern-day novels. Myths to be studied might include Antigone, Oedipus, and Orpheus and Eurydice. (Jr. High)

Boris by Jaap Ter Harr — A twelve year old Russian struggles for survival during the World War II siege of Leningrad in which he looses his mother and his best friend. (Jr. High)

A Farewell to Arms by Ernest Hemingway — Love and war are welded inseparably and tragically in this novel.

To Have and Have Not by Ernest Hemingway — Henry Morgan, who makes a living by rum-running between Florida and Cuba, meets his death.

Hiroshima by John Hersey — This is a compassionate account about survivors of the first atomic bomb.

In the Springtime of the Year by Susan Hill — In her sorrow over her husband's death, this young widow withdraws into solitude. Slowly she is drawn back into the world through the sorrow of others.

The Iliad and *The Odyssey* by Homer — These myths relate the events near the end of the Trojan War and the adventures of one Greek hero as he returns home. Several modern translations are available for young people.

A Sound of Chariots by Mollie Hunter — A young girl growing up in Scotland after World War I tries to come to terms with her grief over her father's death. (Jr. High)

Fog by Mildred Lee — This novel provides an exploration of life and death and the trials of growing up as Luke struggles with teenage conflicts and his father's sudden death.

The Rock and the Willow by Mildred Lee — A young girl growing up in during the Depression in the deep South suffers the loss of a parent. (Jr. High)

Bird on the Wing by Winifred Madison — Elizabeth meets Maija, a weaver, after running away from home. While living with Maija, Elizabeth changes from a shallow schoolgirl to an artist. Maija's sudden death increases Elizabeth's understanding of herself and others.

Teacup Full of Roses by Sharon Bell Mathis — This is a story about Joe, his brothers Paul and David, and his girlfriend. For two years, Joe worked and went to night school so he could go to college. But Paul's drug problems lead to a street fight in which David is killed.

Nilda by Nicholasa Mohr — A ten year old Puerto Rican girl living in New York's Spanish Harlem during World War II loses a parent. (Jr. High)

Poor Jenny, Bright as a Penny by Shirley Murphy — This is a candid portrait of a poor urban family running from one problem to another after the accidental death of the father. Fifteen year old Jenny finds within herself the strength to survive and provide for nine year old Bingo despite the troubles created by Mama and sixteen year old Crystal who dies tragically from drugs.

A Day No Pigs Would Die by Robert Peck — This novel of a Shaker farm boyhood portrays the acceptance of birth, death and the hard work of wrestling a livelihood from the land. In his thirteenth year, the boy becomes a man as he deals with the deaths of a beloved pet and his wise father. (Jr. High)

Chloris and the Creeps by Kim Platt — Eight year old Jenny and her less adaptable eleven year old sister were confused by their parents' divorce and the later suicide of their father. Chloris remains faithful to the father she barely remembers. When her mother remarries, the adjustment for Chloris is psychologically traumatic. (Jr. High)

Changes by Gil Rabin — The move to New York after his father's death brought changes to fourteen year old Chris. Through the support of his first girlfriend, Chris copes with the changes which include his grandfather's failing health and death.

Good Greenwood by Eric Rhodin — The young boy in this novel struggles to adjust to the death of his friend. (Jr. High)

Love Story by Eric Segal — This is a funny-sad story of young love.

Jennifer by Zoa Sherburne — Jennifer and her parents move to Washington state in an attempt to make a new life after the death of Jennifer's twin sister and her mother's subsequent mental breakdown. After a long struggle, Jennifer begins to develop roots in their new home.

By the Highway Home by Mary Stolz — Thirteen year old Catty struggles to understand her brother's death in Vietnam, adjust to a new home, and get along with her self-centered sister. (Jr. High)

The Edge of Next Year by Mary Stolz — After the mother in this story is killed in an automobile accident, the father and two teenage sons experience the suffering of grief in their individual ways.

The Cay by Theodore Taylor — A young white boy and an old black man, who eventually dies, are marooned on an unchartered island. (Jr. High)

Run Softly, Go Fast by Barbara Wersba — On the day of his father's funeral, nineteen year old David begins a diary to examine the father-son estrangement.

The Bridge of San Luis Rey by Thorton Wilder — Two centuries ago in Lima, Peru a willow bridge broke and five people were killed. A monk who witnessed the catastrophe makes a searching study and finds that the lives of these five people had touched one another.

The Summer Before by Patricia Windsor — After the death of her best friend, a teenager tries to relate to a psychiatrist, and also to parents who do not understand her. It is only by keeping a journal that she is able to express her nightmare world and painfully emerge from isolation.

Please Don't Go by Peggy Woodford — Mary's first summer in France with her exchange friend was interesting. The surprise visit to London the following winter by one of the boys suddenly gave promise to a second summer. But the return visit to France ends in sudden tragedy.

The Pigman by Paul Zindel — This novel explores the relationship of two teenagers with an old man and some unfortunate situations. (Jr. High)

Plays:

The Trojan Women by Euripides — The substance of this Greek tragedy is the talk of several women as they wait to be shipped off to slavery after the deaths of their husbands in a war on their town.

Hamlet by William Shakespeare.

Macbeth by William Shakespeare.

Romeo and Juliet by William Shakespeare.

Our Town by Thorton Wilder — This three act play is an attempt to find value for the smallest events in daily life.

You may want to refer to the appendices for suggestions on implementing these works.

Learning Opportunity:
Death in the Visual Arts

Objectives:
- To study the changing view of death as reflected in the progression of art history.

Activities:
Death has been a continuing theme in art forms throughout the centuries. The following basic progression could form an outline for examination.

1. Pre-historical
2. Egyptian
3. Greco-Roman
4. Byzantine
5. Romanesque
6. Gothic
7. Renaissance
8. Baroque
9. Neo-Classical/Romanticism
10. Realism/Impressionism
11. Post Impressionism
12. 20th Century

Students could create their own paintings, collages, etc. which reflect their feelings on death.

Notes to Teacher:
There are an endless number of paintings, pieces of sculpture, etc. which were inspired by an artist's thoughts on death. Use resources which are available to you and encourage students to express their reactions to the subject of the piece of art as well as to the manner in which it is presented.

See "Modern Art and Death" by Carla Gottlieb in *The Meaning of Death* by Herman Feifel (New York: McGraw-Hill, 1959). This chapter includes black and white reproductions of eighteen works of art. There are other topical books, such as *Death in the Middle Ages* by Thomas S.R. Boase (London: Thames and Hudson, 1972), which explore historical areas in fuller detail, as well as general art history survey books like H.W. Jansen's *History of Art* (reprinted, New York: Harry N. Abrams, Inc. and New Jersey: Prentice-Hall, Inc., 1971) which will be useful.

Concept: Attitudes Toward Death and Dying ✌

Learning Opportunity:
Attitudes Toward Death in Literature

Objectives:
- To study attitudes toward death as they are expressed in literature.

Activities:
Read from the following literary works. You may choose to enact selected passages in the classroom. Discuss the attitudes of the characters toward death. What would your attitude have been in the same situation?

The Sandbox by Edward Albee — This sadly comical play portrays a foolish middle aged couple who take Grandmother to the beach to die. Grandmother is humorously resigned to death.

The High and the Mighty by Ernest K. Gann — Twenty people on a Honolulu-to-San Francisco air liner face the strong possibility that the plane will crash. Each person deals with approaching death in an individual manner.

The Man Without a Country by Edward E. Hale — Army Lieutenant Nolan once cursed the United States and was subsequently condemned to spend the remainder of his life on naval vessels. He was never permitted to hear the name of his country until he was dying, an old man at sea.

Bang the Drum Slowly by Mark Harris — This novel centers on a baseball catcher who is dying of Hodgkin's disease and the reactions of his teammates during his last season. There is little sentimentality in the natural and humorous dialogue.

Across the River and Into the Trees by Ernest Hemingway — During the last three days of his life, a fifty year old World War I colonel remembers the crucial events from his near and distant past.

For Whom the Bell Tolls by Ernest Hemingway — This novel about the Spanish Civil War portrays man's courage and his nobility in the face of death.

"Indian Camp" by Ernest Hemingway — In this short story young Nick questions his father about death after uncovering an Indian who had committed suicide.

"The Snows of Kilimanjaro" by Ernest Hemingway — A man considers his imminent death due to gangrene and reflects and hallucinates upon his past.

Zorba the Greek by Nikos Kazantzakis — Zorba contends that his constant awareness of death leads him to a fuller life.

Death from the Sea by Herbert Mason, Jr. — This nonfiction description of the Galveston Hurricane of 1900 which killed thousands of people shows how attitudes toward death and dying may change during a great disaster.

The Godfather by Mario Puzo — This novel takes the reader inside the violence-infested underworld of the Mafia.

Notes to Teacher:

Dear Kids by Lee Wotherspoon (95 Lime St., Newburyport, Mass. 1973) is a poignant journal of a father's letters to his children. Some letters contain his thoughts about his own death and it's possible effect upon his children. His honesty and sincerity make these letters a valuable reference in discussing attitudes about death.

Learning Opportunity:
To Sleep, Perchance

Objective:
• To explore attitudes toward death and dying in poetry.

Activities:
Read and discuss poetry with death themes. The following suggestions are offered:

"The Death of Lincoln" by William Cullen Bryant.

"Thanatopsis" by William Cullen Bryant.

Poetry: A Modern Guide to Its Understanding and Enjoyment by Elizabeth Drew (Death poetry pp. 119-133).

"Resignation" by Henry Wadsworth Longfellow.

"The Wreck of the Hesperus" by Henry Wadsworth Longfellow.

"The Highwayman" by Alfred Noyes
Ariel by Sylvia Plath (confessional poems from the last days of this driven woman's life).
"Annabel Lee" by Edgar Allan Poe.
"Lenore" by Edgar Allan Poe.
"Thou Shalt Not Kill — A Memorial for Dylan Thomas" by Kenneth Rexroth.
The Poems of Dylan Thomas edited by Daniel Jones (102 poems of D. Thomas).
"The Charge of the Light Brigade" by Alfred Lord Tennyson.
The Pocket Book of Modern Prose edited by Oscar Williams.
"Because I Could Not Stop for Death" by Emily Dickinson.
"I Felt a Funeral in My Brain" by Emily Dickinson.
"The Ship of Death" by D. H. Lawrence.
"There, on the Darkened Deathbed" by John Masefield.
"And You as Well Must Die, Beloved Dust" by Edna St. Vincent Millay.
"When I am Dead, My Dearest" by Christina Rossetti.
"A Space in the Air" by Jon Silkin.
"O Captain! My Captain!" by Walt Whitman.
"To Think of Time" by Walt Whitman.

The Great Mother and Other Poems by Michele Murray — Through poetry, Ms. Murray journeys through her ancestry, her childhood, and to her final illness of cancer which took her life at age 40. The last poems, written close to the date of her death, reveal courage and acceptance.

View *Hangman*, a 12 minute film that recreates the nightmare images in the narrative poem of the same title by Maurice Ogden. As the Hangman claims more lives, the scaffold grows to enormous size and the town becomes empty. (McGraw-Hill Films, 1221 Ave. of the Americas, New York, N.Y. 10020)

Notes to Teacher:
You might want to share the following poem written by a fifteen year old.

bury me in blue jeans and a peanuts sweatshirt
    for if i must die, let me do it comfortable.
put my bones in a plywood box and seal the
    lid with elmers glue — to keep bugs out.

or better still burn me in a campfire
   surrounded with echoes of rousing song —
then put me
   in a coffee can to sit on a shelf and watch.
or take my ashes to a tower built of stone
   and scatter them with the wind among gulls . . .
let me fly among the pidgeons and sparrows
   free and light to view everything below
and then set me down, wind, quietly, yet fast
   to the sea to swim forever . . . or just
to the streets, to be ground into traffic
   adding to the clutter.
wherever, blue jeans and peanuts sweatshirt alike,
   just let me die, and then, just for once, be free . . .

Kim Korman, age 15, Framingham, Mass.
from *American Girl*, February, 1971.

Learning Opportunity:
Spoon River Anthology

Objectives:

- To identify personal values about death and what you value in yourself.
- To read an acknowledged masterpiece in American Literature.

Activities:

Read and discuss Edgar Lee Masters' *Spoon River Anthology*. *The New Spoon River* is a sequel to the earlier volume. Both works contain poems that describe the spiritual and physical disintegration of a small American town.

Compose your own epitaph in similar form, describing your character and your manner of death.

Notes to Teacher:

In classroom discussion, focus on the characters and attitudes rather than on formal analysis.

Students may like to dramatize this selection. A good reference is *Development Through Drama* by Brian Way (London: St. Paul's Press, 1967).

Learning Opportunity
Classifications of Death

Objective:
- To study death in several of its temporal interpretations.

Activities:
Death can be described or categorized in numerous ways. Discuss some of the various interpretations in class by viewing death as:

1) Reward — Kamakazie pilots; means of providing insurance money.
2) Punishment — revengeful murders or suicides; capital punishment.
3) Reinforcement of status — use of status symbols in death rituals, e.g., number of flowers, status of pallbearers, quality of casket, size of grave marker; charitable bequests.
4) A means of escape — suicide; escape from responsibilities, e.g., abandonment of aged or infirm, exposure of unwanted children.
5) Entertainment — bullfighting; death-defying sports; hunting for sport; Russian roulette; desire to attend executions.
6) A means of social control — war to protect one's country or to achieve new homeland; destruction to maintain one's community; political executions; capital punishment.

Alternatives to large group discussion would include dividing the class into six discussion groups with each reporting back to the total class or students individually exploring one of these six interpretations and reporting to the class.

Books that would be helpful in studying these interpretations of death include:

The Death Penalty in America edited by Hugo Adam Bedau — This is an anthology of selections by authorities on both sides of disputed questions. There are chapters on capital punishment laws, crimes and executions, arguments for and against the death penalty, and the question of deterrence and abolition.

Death as a Way of Life by Roger Caras — This book on hunting of wildlife presents discussions on hunting techniques throughout the world, the polarization of hunters and anti-hunters in American society, and an argument of firearms control.

Deer Run by Edward Connolly — This novel is a poignant story of the life and violent death of a commune in New England.

The Hessian by Howard Fast — This novel set in the American Revolution expresses the folly of war and the consequences of violence and revenge.

The Lord of the Flies by William Golding — In an attempt to reestablish civilization, young boys stranded on a primitive island while the world is being destroyed revert to savagery and murder.

Death in the Afternoon by Ernest Hemingway — This comprehensive book on Spanish bullfighting includes the historical background, accounts of famed bullfights, photographs and a glossary of terms.

Men at War: The Best War Stories of All Time edited by Ernest Hemingway — This is a collection of 82 stories that tell how men from earliest times have fought and died.

"The Short Happy Life of Francis Macomber" by Ernest Hemingway — More than lions and cape buffalo are killed on this African game safari.

"Sordo's Stand" from *For Whom the Bell Tolls* by Ernest Hemingway — this episode tells of the total defeat of a Resistance band in the Spanish Civil War.

I'm Really dragged But Nothing Gets Me Down by Nat Hentoff — A high school senior is disturbed by deeply conflicting responsibilities to himself, to his family, and to his country as he faces the draft in a time of war.

Soul Catcher by Frank Herbert — In this novel of revenge, an American Indian, outraged by the rape and suicide of his sister, kidnaps a young white boy to sacrifice for murdered innocents among his Indian people.

Capital Punishment, U.S.A. by Elinor Horwitz — The author describes the origins of execution for crime and the renowned cases of the twentieth century which created enormous public reaction and pressure to end capital punishment.

The Last Free Man by Dayton O. Hyde — This book describes the killing of an Indian family in 1911 by a white posse.

Legacy of Death by Barbara Levy — This is a history of a French family whose men served as public executioners for two centuries.

Johnny Got His Gun by Dalton Trumbo — Passionate criticism against senseless death in war is presented by a mutilated soldier who sees himself as the only one ever to come back from the dead.

Build your own learning center on death-defying experiences with task cards focused on various events such as: sports (bullfighting, jousting, tightrope walking, mountain climbing without ropes, sky diving, racing, Evil Knievel); historical happenings (voyages to discover the New World, Lindbergh's transatlantic flight, Byrd's expeditions to the North and South poles); and occupations (fire fighting, bomb squad, undercover narcotic agent). Many items from the *Guiness Book of World Records* could be included.

Learning Opportunity:
Assassination

Objective:
• To study an assassination and it's effect upon the society.

Activity:
Prepare a report on the assassination of a well-known person. Possible choices are: Abraham Lincoln, James Garfield, William McKinley, Medgar Evers, John F. Kennedy, Malcolm X, Martin Luther King, Robert Kennedy, Mrs. Martin Luther King, Sr. and attempted assassinations of Harry Truman, George Wallace and King Hussein. Include in the report a biography of the assassin and a detailed account of the assassination. Violent deaths provide poignant examples for a class discussion which places the end of life in context with a person's growth and accomplishments.

Discuss the possible motivation behind the assassination. How did the general population of the community or country respond? What became of the assassin?

Learning Opportunity:
The Chinese Mandarin Dilemma

Objective:
- To explore the difficulty of making moral judgements related to death.

Activity:
The Chinese Mandarin Dilemma is an ancient question: It goes, "If you know that you had the power to end all the suffering in the world by killing one old Chinese Mandarin in China, would you do it?" You know who and where the man is and there is an absolute certainty that killing him would accomplish the end of suffering in the world. Are there things worth killing for? What does organized religion say to this dilemma? In what situation if any, could you or would you feel justified in killing someone?

Learning Opportunity:
To Die . . .

Objective:
- To reflect upon personal attitudes toward death and dying through analysis of quotations.

Activity:
The following quotations may be used as ideas for group discussion or theme topics:

We begin to die as soon as we are born. (Voltaire)

He who's not busy being born is busy dying. (Bob Dylan)

We don't know life: how can we know death? (Confucius)

In spite of death's endless repetition, it is still not natural. (*View From a Hearse* by Joseph Bayly, Elgin, Ill.: David C. Cook Publ. Co., 1969)

The goal of all life is death. (Sigmund Freud)

. . . In the unconscious every one of us is convinced of his own immortality. (Sigmund Freud)

Death is a punishment to some, to some a gift, and to many a favor. (Senecca)

A single death is a tragedy; a million deaths is a statistic. (Joseph Stalin)

Students may wish to compile a notebook of quotations relating to death. Quotation indexes available in the library's reference department would be useful resources.

In addition to written and oral explanations of the quotations, students might want to illustrate these quotations through cartoons, fingerpainting, collages, etc. Students can attempt to interpret or explain each other's illustrations.

Learning Opportunity:
Dialogue with Death

Objectives:
- To practice the use of imagination as a means to gain understanding about a topic.
- To write a persuasive argument.

Activity:
Imagine a dialogue between you and death, similar to the confrontation between Gramps and Death in the story *On Borrowed Time* by Lawrence Watkin. Write a good argument about why Death should depart with/without you.

Notes to Teacher: This is another good opportunity to mix writing assignments with role-playing and dramatization.

Learning Opportunity:
Count Fosca and Immortality

Objectives:
- To imagine the unknown.
- To consider problems and consequences of immortality.

Activity:
Read the Raymond Fosca story below and then discuss the questions and problems of Count Fosca's predicament.

Count Raymond Fosca, the young and proud ruler of thirteenth century Carmona, was terrified of growing old and dying. The time he had left on earth seemed too tragically short for his realizing anything truly great for the glory of his city. He then met an old man who offered him an elixir of immortality. The old man had discovered it in Egypt but, despite his great fear of death, he dared not drink it. His doubts and fears of a life without end were greater. Count Fosca, on the other hand, had no fear of not dying, especially since the elixir guaranteed him perpetual youth. So he drank the elixir and became immune to death. For two centuries he governed his city, waged wars, constructed new buildings, loved many women, and saw his children, grand-children, and great grand-children die. But lo and behold, he accomplished no more in centuries than he could have in a reign of a few years. His people lived as they pleased and refused to accept their leader's grandiose ideas. Instead of expressing admiration and love, they feared him and wanted to be rid of him. Even his own children thought and acted in terms of their short lives and were not interested in the long range projects of the Count who could not die. After he became painfully aware of this, Count Fosca decided to leave the city of Carmona and became the confidant and evil demon to Emperor Charles V. Unable to achieve his plan of ruling the world, which he had suggested to the Emperor, Fosca then wandered about the world. In the 17th century, he participated in the discovery of Canada. In the 18th century, he was active in the party life of Paris. There, aristocrats and beautiful ladies dreamed of liberty and progress and thus prepared the climate for the horrifying French Revolution. In 1789, Fosca took part in that Revolution, side by side with one of his great grandchildren. He also fought in the revolutions of 1830 and 1848. Fosca was always on the side of the rebels, because they wanted the people to be happy, as he had in 13th century Carmona.

Count Fosca spent years in prison and in exile, and on one occasion slept for sixty years. His wives and children grew old and died, but he always remained the same. Gradually, Fosca became bored and could no longer believe in the future or in progress. Women at first thought that they were exceptionally lucky to be loved by someone immortal, who would always remember them. But they were soon driven to madness when they realized that their immortal lover was unable to give himself to them completely, either in life or in death. And finally, to Count Fosca even the efforts of the most generous man seemed useless to him.[11]

Consider these questions:

As he thought back over his long life, what do you think Count Fosca learned about death and immortality? What difference does the meaning of life have for someone who is immortal and someone who must die? Can someone who is immortal have real emotions? Does life only have meaning for you because you know you will die someday?

Notes to Teacher:

The story is simply a means of introducing the topic of immortality. The problems of immortality described in the story can be contrasted to the glorification of immortality in many works of literature. In what ways do we strive for immortality during our lifetime? (by funding scholarship programs or building monuments in one's name, having children, etc.) There is a chapter dealing with this question in Robert J. Lifton's *Death in Life: Survivors of Hiroshima* (New York: Random House, 1967).

Learning Opportunity:

Childhood Memories

Objectives:

- To communicate an early childhood experience with death through creative art or writing.
- To explore how personal beliefs on death and immortality have changed since early childhood.

---

[11]Adapted from *Death and Its Mysteries* by Ignace Lepp (New York: MacMillan Co. 1968), Chapter 1.

Activities:

Students may use prose, poetry or art (collage, sketch, painting, etc.) to present a personal experience with death during early childhood. The creative communication should portray feelings and thoughts the child had about the dead animal or person and the events surrounding the death.

While sharing these creative expressions in class, students may discuss their ideas about immortality as young children (angels with wings and halos, red devils with pitchforks) and how these ideas have been modified.

Notes to Teacher:

Students should be encouraged to share their personal experiences with death, but it should be generally understood that the student always has the right to pass. Students who do volunteer their experiences may be asked questions of clarification, but probing is to be avoided.

There are several books and articles which discuss the development of children's attitudes toward death. You may want to review some of these and share your findings during student discussion. Suggested teacher resources include:

Anthony, Susan. *The Discovery of Death in Childhood and After.* New York: Basic Books, 1972.

Easson, William M. *The Dying Child — The Management of the Child or Adolescent Who is Dying.* Springfield, Ill.: Charles C. Thomas, 1970.

Grollman, Earl A. *Explaining Death to Children.* Boston: Beacon Press, 1967.

Kliman, Gilbert. *Psychological Emergencies of Childhood.* New York: Grune and Stratton, 1968.

Mitchell, Marjorie E. *The Child's Attitudes Toward Death.* New York: Schocken Books, 1966.

Nagy, Maria. "The Child's View of Death," in *The Meaning of Death.* Ed. by Herman Feifel. New York: McGraw-Hill, 1959.

Vernon, Glenn M. *Sociology of Death — An Analysis of Death Related Behavior.* New York: Ronald Press Co., 1970.

Learning Opportunity:
Death — an Obscenity?

Objective:
- To explore the idea that death is a taboo subject in our culture.

Activities:
Discuss childhood recollections of experiences with death. Consider such questions as: How was death explained to you? What are your earliest memories of exposure to death? Were you allowed to attend the funeral of a friend or family member? Why were you excluded, if you were, and how did you feel?

Question family and friends about death. Consider such questions as: What does life mean in relation to death? Do you think about death very much? This activity could become a total class project through the development of a questionnaire to be given to teenagers and adults. A good resource to use in preparing the questionnaire is the August, 1970 issue of *Psychology Today* which contains a reader questionnaire, "You and Death." See Appendix C for an adaptation of this questionnaire. (The results of this questionnaire appear in the June, 1971 issue.) Students should also be encouraged to develop questions of their own. While tabulating the responses to the questionnaires, note words that are used as substitutes for death, bury, etc. The results of the survey might be published in the school newspaper.

Make a list of words and phrases used as euphenisms for death events. Illustrate some of these using their literal meanings, e.g., bit the dust, kicked the bucket, passed over the hill, carried off into the night.

To dramatize how comfortable students are talking about death, roleplaying may be done in class with the situations written by the teacher or students. Situations might include:

- A four year old asking her teenage brother or sister several questions about death after seeing their dead grandparent in an open casket at a mortuary.

- An elderly person talking about imminent death with a teenage grandchild.

- A teenager going to a funeral home to see a classmate whose parent died unexpectedly.

Notes to Teacher:

To prepare for the first activity on the discussion of childhood recollections, you may find it useful to read Jeffrey Schrank's opening remarks in the chapter on death education in *Teaching Human Beings* (Boston: Beacon Press, 1972). Also, Rose H. Agree and Norman J. Ackerman speak to this subject in "Why Children Must Mourn," *Teacher,* October, 1972, pp. 10, 15-16. See also: Robert Kastenbaum, "The Kingdom Where Nobody Dies," *Saturday Review/Science,* January 1973, pp. 33-38.

Students may be reluctant to roleplay before the entire class. If this is so, they may be divided into small groups with only three to four observers. With several situations being role-played at once, the success of this learning activity will depend upon the involvement of all the students in each small group and their openness to discussing how the players handled the topic of death.

Learning Opportunity:
Death and Television

Objective:
- To survey how death and dying are presented on television.

Activity:
Through group discussions develop a survey form that each student can use while watching television. The survey form should include items that will note violent and natural deaths and the occurrence of a character dying in one program and reappearing later in another program (especially in cartoons).

Also incorporate items that will evaluate the response of other characters in the program to the death. After using the survey form for a selected time period, tabulate and discuss the results.

The class might invite a representative from the local television station to discuss television's role in relaying attitudes toward death.

See *Five Minute Thrill*, a brisk series of violent episodes and murders done in line animation. The interlocking murders are grim fun until one realizes that they resemble the impact of television's menu of violence. (McGraw-Hill Films, 1221 Ave. of the Americas, New York, N.Y. 10020)

Notes to Teacher:
Five Minute Thrill comes with a film guide that includes discussion questions and additional activities.

Learning Opportunity:
Death in Music

Objective:
To study the theme of death as it is presented in popular and classical music.

Activities:
Bring records and tapes to play in the classroom or read lyrics. Each selection should be introduced with information about the composer and the composer's purpose. Discuss how the theme of death (reality, imagery, etc.) is presented in each musical selection.

Study the song "Rock n' Roll Heaven" by the Righteous Brothers. Distribute the lyrics to the class, play the song and discuss the people mentioned: Jimmy Hendrix, Bobby Darin, Jim Morrison, Ottis Reading, Janis Joplin, and Jim Croce. These stars died in various ways — accident, drug abuse, terminal illness, and suicide. Divide into groups to do projects on the life and death of each of these stars. Each group could present their story in any fashion with accompanying music of the star.

Study the song lyrics of "Oh Very Young" by Cat Stevens. Form a list of what each student "would leave us this time."

Discuss "though you think you'll live forever, you know you never will."

Notes to Teacher:
For popular music, rely primarily on the students' knowledge of contemporary lyrics. *Grandfather Rock,* edited by David Morse (New York: Delacorte Press, 1972) has a section on death which compares classical poetry and rock lyrics.

For classical music, the following are possible resources:
"Crucifixus" and "Et Resurrexit" from *B Minor Mass* by J.S. Bach.
"La Mer" by Debussy.
"St. Cecelia's Mass" by Gounod.
Funeral Music by Witold Lutoslowski.
The Funeral March of a Marionette by Pierre.
"Juliet's Death" from *Romeo and Juliet* by Prokofieff.
"Death and Transfiguration" by Strauss.
Petrushka by Igor Stravinsky.
"Siegfried's Funeral Music" from *Gotterdammerung* by Wagner.

Learning Opportunity:
Death on the Screen

Objective:
• To study death as it is presented in American motion pictures.

Activity:
Many of the biggest movie hits with adolescents end with dead heroes or involve the deaths of several persons. Feature films may be used for discussion, reports or critiques. Consider *Bonnie and Clyde, Butch Cassidy, Easy Rider, Godfather, Gone with the Wind, Love Story, Patton, Romeo and Juliet, West Side Story*, or those of the students' own choosing.

Three short films that deal with attitudes about dying are included in a series entitled "Searching for Values / A Film Anthology" from Learning Corporation of America (Film Rental Library, 50-30 Northern Blvd., Long Island City, N.Y. 11101). Each film runs 15 to 17 minutes and was specially edited from a

Columbia Pictures feature motion picture. All of the action
focuses around the specific theme.
Violence: Just for Fun from *Barabbas*. Theme: The thrill of
violence and its fascination for the spectator. Acceptance of
violence.
Love to Kill from *Bless the Beasts and the Children*. Theme:
Hunting and killing for the sake of pleasure. Attitudes toward
killing.
The Right to Live: Who Decides? from *Abandon Ship*. Theme:
The responsibility for decisions about the lives of others. The
dimensions of leadership.

Learning Opportunity:
Grave Humor

Objective:
- To explore how death and death-related events sometimes are
  treated as humorous topics.

Activities:
Explore ways death is dealt with humorously in literature, music,
television, movies, jokes, etc. Are the situations really funny?
Why do we laugh? Do you find yourself laughing even if you do
not think the remark or situation is funny?
Prepare to share and discuss with your classmates a literary
work that deals humorously with a death event. You may want
to select one of the following short stories by Mark Twain:
"At the Funeral" in *Letters From the Earth*.
"Buck Fanshaw's Funeral," "A Dying Man's Confession," "Is
He Living or Is He Dead?," and "The $30,000 Bequest" in
The Complete Short Stories of Mark Twain.
Wills may be humorous as shown in the following excerpts
from *Wills: A Dead Giveaway* by Millie Considine and Ruth
Pool: "Reigning Cats and Dogs," "No Legal Jargon," "Vengeful
Wills," and "A Miscellany of Interesting Wills."
The Loved One by Evelyn Waugh is a short satirical novel
about love and death. Dennis Barlow, a young British poet who
works at a pet cemetery, falls in love with Aimee Thanatogenous,
an American crematorium cosmetician. Humorous contrasts are

made between the pets and the loved ones (the deceased) and the two cemeteries named the Happier Hunting Ground and Whispering Glades.

Another resource is *A Small Book of Grave Humour* by Fritz Spiegel.

Learning Opportunity:
Are These the Facts of Death?

Objective:
• To explore ramifications of death-related events in the hospital environment.

Activity:
Read "The Facts of Death" by Dorothy D. Kates in *Ms.*, February, 1973. This is an account of the death of the author's 100 year old mother who was hospitalized when it became apparent that she was dying. Toward the end of her life, she had to be tied down in order to proceed with life-sustaining treatments.

Notes to Teacher:
Many points of discussion may be raised by this article. Is fighting for someone's life humane in every situation? Why do members of medical staffs seem untouched by the drama of dying? Whose responsibility is it to decide what steps should be taken to prolong life? What alternatives could be offered for this woman's treatment? Why do a larger and larger percentage of people die in institutions? Would you prefer to die at home or in an institution?

A letter to the editor in the May, 1973 issue of *Ms.* offers some provocative responses to this article. Included is the author's reply. These two letters might be useful resources for student discussion.

Learning Opportunity:
Cost of Health Care

Objective:
• To investigate how much it costs to maintain life in a hospital.

Activity:
Contact the business office at a local hospital and explain that you wish to collect data on hospital costs for a school project. The cost of the following items should be included in your request: hospital room, intensive care unit charge, physician services, drugs, daily intravenous feedings, special equipment (heart monitor, respirator), private duty nurse care. You might also ask how much of the hospital bill is paid by insurance coverage on the average.

Notes to Teacher:
This activity may be used as investigative reporting for a journalism project.

Learning Opportunity:
Behind the Sterile Mask

Objective:
- To learn about the role of medical professionals in working with dying people.

Activities:
Invite a physician or nurse to speak with the class. Prepare yourself for the interview before the guest arrives by deciding upon the questions to be asked by each student. Possible questions include:
Have you ever declared a person dead?
How can you tell if a person is dead?
Do you think there is a useable definition of death?
Do you usually tell a terminally ill patient that he/she is going to die? How do you decide?
Do you follow the doctrine "preserve life at all costs?" How does this influence your care of the terminally ill patient?

Notes to Teacher:
The physician or nurse should be informed of the references to which the class has been exposed and their prevailing attitudes toward medical care. Beware of the fact that many physicians are untrained to deal with death as a fact of life because it may be seen as a personal failure.

You may want to look at these resources:

Aronson, Gerald J. "Treatment of the Dying Person," and Kasper August M. "The Doctor and Death," in *The Meaning of Death*, ed. by Herman Feifel (New York: McGraw-Hill, 1959).

Hendin, David. *Death as a Fact of Life*. New York: W.W. Norton & Co., Inc., 1973. See Chapters 1, 4 and 5.

Kates, Dorothy. "The Facts of Death," *Ms.*, Feb., 1973, p. 18.

Ross, Elisabeth K., M.D. "Facing Up to Death," *Today's Education — NEA Journal*, Jan. 1972, pp. 30-32.

Ross, Elizabeth K., M.D. *On Death and Dying*. New York: Macmillan Co., 1969.

"Life, Death and Medicine," *Scientific American*, Sept. 1973 (entire issue).

Sudnow, David, *Passing On*. Englewood Cliffs, N.J.: Prentice-Hall, Inc., 1967.

Learning Opportunity:
The Good Death?

Objectives:
- To respond to an imaginary situation in which the participants might consider whether life is always worth living.
- To use an imaginary situation to consider the possibility of self-involvement in decisions about the time and means of death for self and loved ones.

Activities:
Read "A Question of Love and Death," a play by Arnold Rubin in *Senior Scholastic*, May 2, 1974. In this short three-act dramatization, 18 year old Barry's parents must make a difficult decision after a tragic accident. Select persons for each of the characters and read the play in class.

Role play the process of decision-making that an euthanasia board might experience (including the input of family, lawyer, physician, or others) in the following situations:

1) The mother of a severely deformed baby asks the doctors to terminate life-sustaining procedures on her child.

2) A hospitalized patient with a terminal disease requests to die in peace.

3) A young man asks that he be allowed to die after being told by doctors that he will be completely paralyzed the rest of his life following an accident.

Read "The Courage to Say 'No' " by Jessamyn West in *Family Health*, November, 1974. The writer tells the story of her sister who found the strength to say no to suffering although death due to cancer could not be avoided.

Notes to Teacher:

Discussions generally center on "What if . . .?" and are useful in illustrating the difficulties of this problem. The decision may seem to be more clear-cut if more conditions are attached to the role play example, but conclusive answers are rarely found.

A major theme for discussion is the question, "Should life be preserved at all costs?" Also, you may want to discuss the origin of the word "euthanasia" (Greek for "the good death") and its current usage in the form of "mercy killing."

The following resources may be useful for this and similar activities:

Downing, A.B., ed. *Euthanasia and the Right to Death: The Case for Voluntary Euthanasia*. New York: Humanities Press, 1969.

Fletcher, Joseph. *Morals and Medicine*. Boston: Beacon Press, 1960.

Hendin, David. Chapter 3: "Euthanasia: Let There Be Death," in *Death as a Fact of Life*. New York: W.W. Norton & Co., Inc., 1973.

Maguire, Daniel C. *Death By Choice*. Garden City, N.Y.: Doubleday & Co., 1974.

"Mercy Killers," (30 min.) A BBC Production distributed by Time/Life Films, 43 W. 16th St., New York, N.Y., 10011.

Williams, Glanville. *The Sanctity of Life and the Criminal Law*. New York: A.A. Knopf, 1957.

A provocative film entitled, *Who Should Survive?* may also be used to stimulate thought and group discussion. This 26 minute film contains a dramatic sequence in which a mongoloid infant is allowed to die; following this, a panel of experts discuss ethical, legal, and scientific issues (Medal of Greatness, 1032 33rd Street, N.W., Washington, D.C. 20007).

Learning Opportunity:
Driver's Education

Objective:
- To explore the value of showing films portraying violent death on the highway for the purpose of driver education.

Activity:
See the films *Signal 30, Mechanized Death* or others similar in focus. Discuss the attitudes towards death and dying that we might be instilling in people by showing these movies as a means to encourage safe driving. Discuss the problem of violence on the highways and the apparent lack of concern for the lives of others. How might we encourage safe driving without developing an unhealthy fear of death and dying?

Notes to Teacher:
Do people become better drivers because of the fear instilled by films? Is it more effective to shock and instill fear of death rather than to influence students by other means? Even if it proves effective on the road, is it psychologically healthy?

Concept:
Life Philosophy & Death ✌

Learning Opportunity:
Values Toward Life and Death

Objective:
- To identify and clarify some of one's own values influencing life and death decisions.

Activity:
Divide the class into groups of six or seven persons. Explain the following situation to the groups.

You are members of a government department who are in charge of experimental stations in the far reaches of civilization. Suddenly a world war breaks out and the bombing begins. You receive a desperate call from one of your stations requesting help. The situation there is as follows: There are ten people but only enough space, air, food and water in their fall-out shelter for six people to survive for three months. In order to avoid fighting among themselves, they have requested that you, their superiors, decide which four of the ten will have to be eliminated from the shelter. You must act quickly because you have only twenty minutes before you must enter your own fall-out shelter. Keep in mind that it is entirely possible that the six persons you select to remain in the fall-out shelter may be the only six survivors remaining to start the human race over again. Therefore, the choice is important: do not let yourself be pressured by the other group members. Try to make the best selection possible based upon this superficial description of the ten people: 1) a 31 year old accountant; 2) his wife who is six months pregnant; 3) a black militant who is a second year medical student; 4) a 42 year old famous historian-author; 5) a 26 year old Hollywood starlette; 6) a 62 year old bio-chemist; 7) a 54 year old Rabbi; 8) an Olympic athlete who excells in several sports; 9) a college co-ed majoring in education; 10) a policeman who insists on wearing his gun.

Hand out lists of these descriptions and tell the groups to begin. They are to stop in exactly twenty minutes with their decision reached.[12]

Discuss how you made your decisions. What values seem to be important? Consider variations of the ten people who could be in the same predicament or imagine a similar situation.

Learning Opportunity:
Not Many Tomorrows

Objective:
- To explore the relationship between knowledge of one's own impending death and questions concerning life accomplishments and self-fulfillment.

Activities:
Read a story about someone who knew he/she did not have long to live. How did this person behave in the last months of life? Does the story provoke an increased consciousness of your own mortality? What are your thoughts and feelings about a shortened life? Stories that you might use for this activity include:

Admission to the Feast by Gunnel Beckman — Nineteen year old Annika faces the knowledge that she is going to die from leukemia. In a letter to a friend she reviews the circumstances of her life and the meaning of life and death.

The Sparrow's Fall by Fred Bodsworth — In his battle against starvation, a Canadian Indian discovers the nobility of life in face of nature's violence.

I Heard the Owl Call My Name by Margaret Craven — With three years to live, a 27 year old missionary is sent to an Indian village in Canada where he learns the primitive meaning of life and death.

For Love of Anne by Claude deLeusse — Anne died in Paris of a rare incurable illness when she was fifteen. Anne's mother tells the story of the family's life and courage during Anne's thirteen and a half years of illness.

---

[12]Adapted from Sidney B. Simon, et al., *Values Clarification* (New York: Hart, 1972), pp. 281-283.

Doctor Tom Dooley, My Story — Dr. Dooley tells about his life and his fatal fight against cancer.

The Diary of a Young Girl by Anne Frank — This book demonstrates how magnificently the spirit of a young girl can ignore the shadow of death and an almost impossible way of life.

Death Be Not Proud by John Gunther — This is the true struggle of a seventeen year old boy's losing battle against a brain tumor.

Sunshine by Norma Klein — This is a true story of twenty year old Jacquelyn Helton who died in 1971 of bone cancer. In the last 18 months of life, she kept a tape-recorded diary as a legacy for her daughter. (A story-interview appears in *Today's Health*, December, 1971 entitled "Brave Young Mother" by Mike Michaelson.)

Eric by Doris Lund — This true story of a seventeen year old's tragic fight against leukemia is told by his mother.

A Short Season by Jean Morris — This reveals the life story of Brian Piccolo, a running back for the Chicago Bears, who died from cancer at the height of his football career.

Alive: The Story of the Andes Survivors by Piers Paul Read — This is the true story of a group of men and women who took off on a flight from Uruguay to Chile. When their plane hit a mountain, some passengers died immediately and others lingered with injuries. When food ran out, it was necessary to use the bodies of the deceased for nutrition. After more than two months, two men finally walk down the mountain to seek rescue.

How Could I Not Be Among You by Ted Rosenthal — At the age of thirty, Rosenthal was told that he had leukemia. This book comes from the words he wrote and spoke in the last months of his life.

Films appropriate for this activity are:

How Could I Not Be Among You (28 min.) — This is an intimate portrait of a young man who has been told he has six months to live. (Eccentric Circle Cinema Worshop, Box 1481, Evanston, Ill. 60204).

You See — I've Had a Life (30 min.) — A thirteen year old all-American boy has leukemia and his family seeks to share the realities of his illness. (Eccentric Circle Cinema Workshop, Box 1481, Evanston, Ill. 60204).

Occurrence at Owl Creek (27 min.) — The heightened awareness of a man about to be hanged is depicted. (Visual Aids Service Division of Univ. Extension, University of Illinois, Champagne, Ill. 61822).

Soon There Will Be No More Me (10 min.) A young mother facing death speaks of her doubts and fears and of her values on life (Churchill Films, 662 N. Robertson Blvd., Los Angeles, Calif. 90069).

Create an artistic poster that says "Will it matter that I was?" Students may express their reactions verbally and artistically.

Learning Opportunity:
Are There Things Worth Dying For?

Objective:
• To explore the value of dying for a committment to a cause.

Activities:
The following four plays may be used to stimulate a discussion on martyrdom. Students may wish to practice the parts and then set up a simple "kitchen stools and spotlights" stage in an unused auditorium to enact selected scenes.

Becket or The Honor of God by Jean Anouilk; *Murder in the Cathedral* by Thomas S. Eliot — Both of these plays portray the the clash of wills between Thomas a Becket, Archbishop of Canterbury and his antagonist-friend, King Henry II.

A Man for All Seasons by Robert Bolt — In an act of conscience, Thomas More as Archbishop of Canterbury defies King Henry VIII.

Saint Joan by George Bernard Shaw — This play presents the last two years of Joan of Arc's life.

Notes to Teacher:
Students could also read some of the numerous articles and books that have been written about Martin Luther King who was assassinated in 1968 and/or the four students killed at Kent State University in 1970. Although these individuals did not intend to die for their cause, what was the effect of their deaths? Have they become martyrs?

To explore the combined political and religious perspectives of dying for a cause, consider the inconsistency between the goals of Christianity and fighting between the Catholics and Protestants in Ireland. Students might read *Exodus* by Leon M. Uris which describes people in mortal struggle to establish a homeland in Israel and live in freedom.

Invite a local military recruiter to discuss with the class the Armed Services' attitude towards dying, death education, and the value of life. In addition, a military chaplain could lead a discussion on the attitudes held by conscientious objectors . . . and roles which some objectors have performed during war time (e.g., ambulance drivers, medical orderlies, and other helpful non-combatant roles).

Learning Opportunity:
Is Death the End?

Objective:
- To explore various answers to the question, what happens after death?

Activities:
The following two books of fantasy may stimulate your thinking on this subject:

Jonathan Livingston Seagull by Richard Bach — Jonathan's understanding of things unseen and unimagined enables him to transcend the here and now of life.

The Little Prince by Antoine de Saint-Exupery — The Little Prince lived alone on a tiny planet with a beautiful flower. It was the pride of this flower that started the Little Prince on travels that brought him at last to Earth where he finally learned the secret of what is really important in life.

Have a class discussion to share personal beliefs concerning the human soul or spirit after death. A poll might be taken among your friends to see how many people believe in some form of life after death.

Interview persons with various philosophical and religious beliefs about life after death. Share your findings in class.

The class should be assured that the aim of discussions for this opportunity is not to achieve a consensus, but to share diverse feelings and interpretations.

An interesting resource is Suzy Smith's book, *Life Is Forever — Evidence for Survival After Death* (New York: G.P. Putnam's Sons, 1974). Ms. Smith, a renowned psychic, deals with mysteries of the hereafter using examples of beyond-the-grave communications.

Learning Opportunity:
Frozen Smile

Objective:
- To explore the implications of cryogenic freezing for the individual, the family, and society.

Activity:
Science has developed a method of quick freezing bodies in the hope that they can be thawed at a later time if and when the cause of the person's death becomes curable. Thus, the thawed person would be repaired and could then continue life. If someone was murdered and then frozen with every possibility of being brought back to life, is that person really dead? Should the "murderer" be tried for manslaughter? How much do you think it costs to be frozen and kept in a frozen state? Do you think freezing will become widespread in the foreseeable future? Will our society condone the practice of cryogenic freezing? What advantages and complications may occur? Imagine yourself in such a situation, i.e., never dying. Does cryogenics represent extreme selfishness or is it an act of self-preservation?

Notes to Teacher:
Write to the Life Extension Society, 2011 N. Street, Washington, D.C. 20036 for free information on cryonics. Also write to Cryonics Society of New York, Inc., 9 Holmes Court, Sayville, L.I., N.Y. 11782.

While you are waiting for the return mail, look at these books:
Ettiger, Robert C.W. *The Prospect of Immortality*. New York: MacFadden, 1969.

Hendin, David. Chapter 8: "Death and the Deep Freeze," in *Death as a Fact of life*. New York: W. W. Norton & Co., 1973.
Nelson, Robert. *We Froze the First Man*. New York: Dell, 1968.

A report about cryogenics, appeared on page 20 of the *Chicago Tribune* on Sunday, April 6, 1975. Robert Ettinger stated 24 people had been frozen in the ten year history of cryogenics; some of those have since been thawed and buried. Cryogenic freezing costs about $15,000 for initial expenses and $1800 a year for maintenance in a capsule of liquid nitrogen at 320 degrees below zero.

Learning Opportunity:
Death in the Future

Objective:
● To fantasize about changes in death and dying in the twenty-first century.

Activities:
Read a science fiction work that comments about death and dying beyond the year 2000. One of the following stories by Robert Silverberg may be selected:

Recalled to Life is set in 2033. A research organization has developed a process whereby scientists can reanimate people who have been dead less than 24 hours if no major organ damage has occurred. After the public announcement of the life-restoring process, a bitter debate erupts across the United States.

Born with the Dead contains three novellas about the spirit of man. In "Born with the Dead," the hereafter totally occupies the imagination of a man who has lost his wife, but he finally becomes indifferent to her after his own death. "Going" is a study of one man's mortality in a nation where each individual may pick the moment he chooses to die.

Another possible resource is *Going* by Sumner Locke Elliott. The heroine of this story, 65 years of age, is faced with euthanasia which is the form of Medicare meted out to the elderly in this future time.

Share the science fiction experiences with your classmates. Discuss whether these ideas seem possible in the next few decades. Are these ideas based upon an acceptance of death in the future or do they perpetuate denial of death?

Concept: Death Rituals ✌

Learning Opportunity:
Death and the Law

Objective:
- To study some of the legal issues involved in death.

Activities:
Read the Kansas Statute on Death (see below). Can Legislators really decide when someone is dead? What are the civil rights of dying people? Discuss in groups and write your own law.

Kansas Statute on Death

A person will be considered medically and legally dead, if in the opinion of a physician, based on ordinary standards of medical practice, there is the absence of spontaneous respiratory and cardiac function and, because of the disease or condition which caused directly or indirectly, these functions to cease, or because of the passage of time since these functions ceased, attempts at resuscitation are considered hopeless; and, in this event, death will have occurred at the time these functions ceased; or

A person will be considered medically and legally dead if, in the opinion of a physician, based on ordinary standards of medical practice, there is the absence of spontaneous brain function; and if based on ordinary standards of medical practice, during reasonable attempts to either maintain or restore spontaneous circulatory or respiratory function in the absence of aforesaid brain function, it appears that further attempts at resuscitation or supportive maintenance will not succeed, death will have occurred at the time when these conditions first coincide. Death is to be pronounced before artificial means of supporting respiratory and circulatory function are terminated and before any vital organ is removed for purpose of transplantation.

These alternative definitions of death are to be utilized for all purposes in this state, including the trials of civil and criminal cases, any laws to the contrary notwithstanding. (Kansas State Legislature, Topeka, Kansas)

Read parts of the State Sanitary Code which contains the laws for the transportation of dead bodies, for cremation, for death and burial permits, etc. Write down your reactons. Do any laws need changing?

Fill out a reproduction of a death certificate imagining the circumstances of your death. What information is requested?

Notes to Teacher:
Death certificate forms are available from your local coroner's office.

After four years (1971-75) of studying more than 500 dying patients in nine medical centers across the country, medical experts from the American Medical Association (A.M.A.) have created a new medical definition of death which they feel confident fulfills all moral, ethical, and legal requirements. Under the new definition a person may safely be declared dead "if he is in a coma, has no brain activity as measured by an electroencephlagraph, he has no reactions such as swallowing, coughing, and pupillary movement, his pupils remain large, he has a temperature below 90 degrees, and there is no clinical or chemical evidence of drug intoxication." (Source: Kotulak, Ronald. "Death definition meets test of life," *Chicago Tribune*, Feb. 2, 1975).

In March 1975 the legal profession also revised its definition of death which had stood unchanged since 1906 (a person is legally dead when his breathing and heart beat has stopped). It took the 180-member committee of the American Bar Association's (A.B.A.) Medicine and Law Section 18 months and at a cost of $200,000 to arrive at its current definition of death: "For all legal purposes, a human body with irreversible cessation of total brain function, according to usual and customary standards of medical practice, shall be considered dead." (Source: Kotulak, Ronald. "Doctors bar work toward legal definition of death," *Chicago Tribune*, March 9, 1975.)

According to Edwin Holman, A.M.A. attorney, the new definition of the A.B.A. appears to coincide with the policies of the American Medical Association.

Learning Opportunity:
Autopsy

Objectives:
- To study the major purposes of autopsy.
- To identify how permission for autopsy is obtained.

Activities:
Read "How Post-Mortems Help the Living" by Norman M. Lobsenz in the May, 1972 issue of *Today's Health.* (A condensation of this article, "How Autopsies Save Lives," appears in the October, 1973 issue of *Reader's Digest.*) This article discusses seven major purposes of autopsy which is one of the most important methods of learning about disease.

Obtain an autopsy consent form from a local hospital. Study it to see the kind of information requested. Discuss how you would feel about signing such a consent. What are the reasons for your position? Might individual circumstances about the death affect your decision?

A physician may be invited to speak with the class about the purposes of autopsy and how the results are shared with the deceased's family.

Learning Opportunity:
Obituaries

Objective:
- To evaluate the appropriateness and style of obituaries.

Activities:
Read the obituary columns in one local and one major newspaper. Compare their style and content. If you think they need improvement or could be better, create one of your own.

Write your own obituary as it might appear if you were to die suddenly. You may choose any age to write about and can fantasize about what your accomplishments might be (or are) at the time. Make your obituary as long as you want and include in it all the things that are unique and worthy of being remembered. The ritual of remembering is really a celebration of life.

To supplement this activity, you might ask the news reporter who writes the obituary columns to speak to your class. How does he/she like the job? Why?

Read to the class or make copies of Jessica Mitford's few pages dealing with the obituary columns in her book, *The American Way of Death* (New York: Fawcett-World, 1969). This is a provocative report which can be useful in starting discussions and debates.

Learning Opportunity:
Death American Style

Objectives:
- To explore different opinions held by individuals and groups on American death rituals.
- To become aware of advertising and sales techniques in the funeral business.

Activities:
Books dealing with American death rituals that may be read include:

The High Cost of Dying by Ruth Harmer — The major thrusts of this book include the advocacy of reductions in funeral costs and the replacement of funerals with memorial societies.

The American Way of Death by Jessica Mitford — This humorous and satirical book exposes the hypocrisy of modern funerals.

The Funeral: Vestige or Value? by Paul E. Irion — Several chapters in this book could serve as a stimulus for personal reflection and/or group discussion. Chapter topics include the American attitudes toward death, a multidimensional definition for funeral, an evaluation of the funeral according to given norms, and proposals for new designs.

A Manual of Death Education and Simple Burial by Ernest Morgan — This booklet has information on donorship, wills, simple burial and cremation. It also includes addresses on death-related organizations and resources such as films, sample documents (donor cards, living will), checklists, etc.

Interview one or more of the following persons who has a role in the funeral business: mortician, salesman of grave markers or burial plots, florist or memorial society representative. As a class, write the questions you want answered by each interviewee. Take notes on opinions and positions stated during the interviews. Be sure to distinguish fact from opinion. Share your findings with the class. Discuss how the goal to affirm the reality of death through the death ritual can be achieved without overemphasizing the ritual itself. Do individuals have the right to determine what kind of funeral, if any, they want for themselves when the purpose of the funeral is to support the living?

Arrange for interested students to visit a funeral home to tour the facilities. Look at magazines of the trade, a sample funeral pre-arrangement form, varieties in style, quality and prices of caskets and vaults, etc. If this cannot be arranged, you may ask a mortician to be a guest speaker for the class.

Notes to Teacher:

A funeral is the third largest lifetime expenditure (after a house and a car) for the average person, but it is unlikely that he/she will have discussed the funeral with anyone before dying. Moreover, every individual will probably share the responsibility of arranging for at least one funeral for a relative. Therefore, an opportunity to visit a funeral home and talk with a mortician should be beneficial for students.

The National Funeral Directors Association (135 Wells St., Milwaukee, Wisc. 53203) publishes a bibliography of pamphlets, journals and books available for purchase and audiovisual materials available for purchase and rental. You could ask your local funeral directors if they have any educational materials available to give students. With advance notice, a mortician might also assist you in selecting and showing one of the films. A film entitled, "Too Personal to be Private" is highly recommended.

Two other fraternal organizations that might provide additional resources are the International Order of the Golden Rule (726 S. College St., Springfield, Ill.) and the National Selected Morticians (1616 Central St., Evanston, Ill. 60201).

Requests for information about memorial societies may be sent to the Continental Association of Funeral and Memorial Societies (Suite 1100, 1828 L. St. N.W., Washington, D.C. 20036). This is the central office for several hundred local associations which seek to simplify the funeral ritual and to assist people to pre-plan for their funerals so their relatives will not be left to do it in a rush when they are grieving.

Learning Opportunity:
History in the Graveyard

Objectives:
- To study burial practices as an aspect of American History.
- To compare early burial practices with contemporary practices.
- To find history and art lessons in a graveyard.

Activities:
Investigate the burial practices during the colonial period and early American History (post-1776), tracing those that are carried over to today in unchanged form, including gravestone writings and perhaps gravestone "poetry." The self determination possible in an earlier period of society, when a person could be prepared for burial by the family and placed under a tree on the family farm, may be contrasted with the controls established by contemporary health agencies. A mortician may serve as a guest speaker to discuss the regulations regarding body preparation and burial in cemeteries.

Graveyard sculpture, tombs and epitaphs can reveal much about the history of America and your local area. Books of interest include:

A Book of Epitaphs by Raymond Lamont Brown.
Early New England Gravestone Rubbings by Edmond V. Gillon
Graven Images by Allen Ludwig
Over Their Dead Bodies: Yankee Epitaphs & History by Thomas C. Mann and Janet Greene
American Epitaphs, Grave and Humorous by Charles L. Wallis

Take shelf paper, rubbing wax, masking tape, scissors, paper and pen to the oldest graveyard in your area. Make rubbings and

collect epitaphs, trying to gather a representative and chrono-
logical sample of those available to you. Note the stylistic changes
in both the gravemarkers and the epitaphs. Do you see any
"Death's Heads," cherubs, or urns and willows? Do the epitaphs
say "Here lies the body of . . ." which stresses decay of the body
or do they say "In the Memory of . . ." which emphasizes eternal
life? What do the graveyard findings reflect about this history
of your area?

Notes to Teacher:
You may send for *The Residents of Tombstone's Boot Hill* by
Ben Traywick and *So Said the Coroner* by Grace McCool by
writing The Tombstone Epitaph, Tombstone, Ariz. 85638 and
sending $2.50 for each book plus 25c for mailing.

Learning Opportunity:
Ashes to Ashes

Objective:
• To study cremation as an alternative to traditional burial.

Activities:
Read Chapter 11: "Cremation" in *The American Way of Death*
by Jessica Mitford. Discuss cremation as an alternative to
traditional burial practices. Who makes decisions as to what can
or should be done with the deceased's body? May you as an
individual request to be cremated after you die, even though
you know your family does not favor cremation?

Read "Light, Like the Sun" by Frances Newton in the March,
1974 issue of *The Readers Digest* (pp. 153-157). This memorable
article, printed for the third time, describes a personal experience
about the question of burial versus cremation.

The Rose Tatoo, a play by Tennessee Williams, permits
discussion of Serafina's decision to cremate her husband's body
despite the priest's opinion. Discussion could include cultural
contrasts such as public cremation in India witnessed by young
children amid the support of kin.

A mortician may be invited as a guest speaker to present the
technical aspects of cremation. Prepare questions you would like

answered. Interested students might visit the crematory if there is one in your community.

Notes to Teacher:
You may wish to read Chapter 9: "Make Way for the Living" in *Death as a Fact of Life* by David Hendin (New York: W.W. Norton, 1973).

Learning Opportunity:
Organized Religion and Death

Objectives:
- To identify the death beliefs, customs and rituals of organized religions.
- To meet the clergy from religions and denominations other than your own.

Activities:
As a class, prepare questions to ask clergymen about death beliefs, customs and rituals of their respective religions and denominations. Interview a representative sample, or perhaps all, of the clergy in your community. Compare and contrast your findings in class.

Prepare a report on the death beliefs and rituals of one of the world's major religions. The class may be divided into groups to be sure that major religions (Buddhism, Christianity, Hinduism, Judaism, Muhammedanism, Shintoism and Zoroastrianism) will be included.

Notes to Teacher:
The students also could solicit reactions from the clergy about the value of death education in schools and any suggestions they might have for additional activities.

Students may use periodicals as well as reference books in preparing their reports on death beliefs and rituals of world religions. For example, a pictorial essay on death rites of Hinduism entitled "The Ganges, River of Faith" by John J. Putman appears in the October 1971 issue of *National Geographic* (pages 445-483).

Learning Opportunity:
Death in Other Cultures

Objectives:
- To study death beliefs, customs, and rituals in other cultures.
- To appreciate that death practices in other cultures are meaningful to those persons.

Activities:
Independently study the death beliefs and practices of another culture and report your findings to the class. You may use the following resources:

Douglass, William A. *Death in Murelaga.* Seattle: University of Washington Press, 1969. (Basque community in Northern Spain).

Goody, Jack. *Death, Property and the Ancestors.* Stanford, Calif.: Stanford Univ. Press, 1962. (Lo Daga tribe in Ghana)

Habenstein, Robert W. and Lamers, William M. *Funeral Customs the World Over.* Milwaukee: Bulfin Printers, 1963.

Malinowski, Bronislaw. *Magic, Science and Religion.* Garden City, N.Y.: Doubleday & Co., 1954. (Trobriand Islanders)

Mandlebaum, David G. "Social Uses of Funeral Rites" in *The Meaning of Death,* ed. by Herman Feifel. New York: McGraw-Hill, 1959. (Kota of South India, Cocopa, Hopi and Apache Indians, the Scottish Island of Barra, and Java)

Meyer, Pamela and Alfred. "Life and Death in Tana Toradja" in *National Geographic,* June, 1972. (Indonesia).

Notes to Teacher:
Read Chapter 8: "Funerals," in A. Van Gennup's *The Rites of Passage* (Chicago: Univ. of Chicago Press, 1960). Van Gennup's theory is that the rituals performed during "life crisis" includes rites of separation, transition, and incorporation.

You might show the film *Dead Birds* (21 min.) which depicts beliefs of a New Guinea tribe on death, war, revenge, and spirits that are foreign to American beliefs. (Audiovisual Center, University of Indiana, Bloomington, Indiana 47401).

Concept: Preparation for Personal Death

Learning Opportunity:
Is Life a Safe Bet?

Objectives:
- To study the history of life insurance, one of America's most pervasive social institutions.
- To recognize the mathematics and economics involved in buying and selling life insurance.
- To identify different psychological motivations for purchasing life insurance.

Activities:
Investigate the history of life insurance. Why is it an important and well established part of American life?

Invite a life insurance agent or executive to speak to the class. Why/how does an insurance company make a profit? Why wasn't there any life insurance 100-150 years ago? What are the relationships between "modern living" and life insurance? Why isn't it called death insurance? Are there differences — cost, type, amount of coverage, etc. — in life insurance purchased by men and women? What are the reasons for the differences? At what age should life insurance be purchased? How much does it cost? Why have life insurance if you have no living relatives?

Interview adult friends (male and female) concerning their reasons for purchasing life insurance and the factors they considered when selecting the amount of coverage. Discuss your findings in class.

Notes to Teacher:
In the context of education, the value of a class visit by an insurance agent (or any other person working in occupations that have direct or peripheral involvement with death) is in enabling students to explore and to talk openly about the impact of death in many occupations in our society.

Learning Opportunity:
I Hereby Bequeath

Objectives:
- To study the value of a will in property settlement.
- To learn when and how to make a will.

Activities:
Invite a lawyer to speak with the class. Before the lawyer comes, identify questions about wills you would like answered. These are some suggestions: What is a will? Does a married woman need a will? How do you make one? How much does it cost? What if you want to change it? Where is the will kept? Do you need a will if you do not own real estate?

Take a poll to see how many parents and grandparents of students in the class have a will. What reasons do they give for having/not having a will?

Wills: A Dead Giveaway by Millie Considine and Ruth Pool contains an array of wills of some of the world's most interesting testators. People express everything from love and gratitude to vengeance and graveyard humor in the wills cited in this book.

Notes to Teacher:
Although most young adults do not have many personal assets in the first few years after graduation, a class discussion about wills and how they facilitate property settlement might influence a later decision. The students might also want to encourage their parents and other relatives to make a will.

Showing the film *Wrong Box* would initiate a discussion of property settlement in a comical manner. This is a hilarious account of a family who agreed to bequeath the family fortune to the last survivor. The movie depicts the connivings of family members to be the last survivor. (Columbia Films, 711 Fifth Avenue, New York City, N.Y. 10022)

Learning Opportunity:
A Living Will

Objective:
- To explore feelings about maintaining life in the event of one's own irreversible illness.

Activity:
A lively class discussion might be started on the topic of a "living will." This is a formal request prepared by the Euthanasia Educational Council that informs the signer's family or others who may be concerned with the signer's wish to avoid the use of "heroic measures" to maintain life in the event of irreversible illness. The text of this document is reproduced below:

TO MY FAMILY, MY PHYSICIAN,
MY CLERGYMAN, MY LAWYER —
If the time comes when I can no longer take part in decisions for my own future, let this statement stand as the testament of my wishes:
If there is no reasonable expectation of my recovery from physical or mental disability, I, _____
request that I be allowed to die and not be kept alive by artificial means or heroic measures. Death is as much a reality as birth, growth, maturity and old age — it is the one certainty. I do not fear death as much as I fear the indignity of deterioration, dependence and hopeless pain. I ask that medication be mercifully administered to me for terminal suffering even if it hastens the moment of death.
This request is made after careful consideration. Although this document is not legally binding, you who care for me will, I hope, feel morally bound to follow its mandate. I recognize that it places a heavy burden of responsibility upon you, and it is with the intention of sharing that responsibility and of mitigating any feelings of guilt that this statement is made.

Notes to Teacher:
Information about the living will and copies of it may be obtained free by writing the Euthanasia Educational Council, 250 West 57th, New York, New York 10019.
A useful resource for this activity is Chapter 3: "Euthanasia: Let There Be Death" in *Death as a Fact of Life* by David Hendin (New York: W.W. Norton & Co., Inc., 1973).

Learning Opportunity:
A Living Bank

Objectives:
- To discuss the pros and cons of donorship of body parts after death.
- To learn how a person can arrange for posthumous donations of body parts for transplants or research.

Activities:
Read true stories reported in popular magazines about persons whose body parts were donated after death for others. The class may wish to arrange for a debate with one team supporting the stand that donorship by the deceased's next-of-kin is heartless while the other team argues that donorship ensures that the death of one person prolongs the life of another.

The Living Bank is a non-profit organization dedicated to helping persons who wish to donate a part or all parts of their bodies after death for the purposes of transplantation, medical research or anatomical studies. The Living Bank explains the procedure and provides a donor registration form in addition to a Uniform Donor Card which is the only legal document needed under the Uniform Anatomical Gift Act. The text of the Uniform Donor Card is reproduced below:

In the hope that I may help others, I hereby make this anatomical gift, if medically acceptable, to take effect upon my death. The words and marks below indicate my desires.

I give:
(a)   any needed organs or parts
(b)   only the following organs or parts

_____

    Specify which organ(s) or part(s) for the purposes of transplantation, therapy, medical or education;
(c)   my body for anatomical study if needed.

Limitations or special wishes, if any: _____

Signed by the Donor and two witnesses in the presence of each other.

Notes to Teacher:
Donorship of body parts, both by the deceased's family and by the individual's previously arranged plans, is becoming more popular. Diversity of student views on this issue can help them understand the failure of kin to agree on decisions that may have to be made during their bereavement. The class should be informed that the aim of discussion is not consensus but a sharing of diverse feelings and interpretations. Students may be concerned about the moral issues surrounding donation of body parts. This potential discussion merits your prior consideration.

Information about the Living Bank and copies of the Uniform Donor Card may be obtained free by writing the Living Bank, 6631 S. Main St., Houston, Texas 77005.

The National Kidney Foundation also will send information about donating body parts to science. Their address is 315 Park Ave. South, New York, N.Y. 10010.

For information about eye donation and guidance to the nearest eye bank contact the International Eye Foundation, Sibley Memorial Hospital, Washington, D.C.

David Hendin discusses donorship of the human body for transplantation of organs and anatomical study in Chapter 2: "Transplants, You Can Take It With You" in *Death as a Fact of Life* (New York: W.W. Norton & Co., Inc., 1973).

Learning Opportunity:
Attend Your Own Funeral

Objectives:
- To experience a group fantasy concerning death.
- To act out one's feelings about death.

Activity:
Lie down on your back, placing your hands at your sides. Imagine your life has left you. Close your eyes, do not move or

speak. You are in a funeral parlor and people are coming to see you. How are you dressed? Look at the faces of the people above you. Who is there? How are they feeling? What does each one say? Is there someone there that is glad that you are dead? Is there someone there who envies your being dead? Select some of the people who come to see you and say something to them (do this silently). In other words, if you could speak to people for the last time and had absolutely nothing to fear from them, what would you say? What music is being played? Someone is giving your eulogy; what is being said? What would you like the person to say?

Notes to Teacher:
This activity should only be undertaken if you, the teacher, feel comfortable monitoring this experience. Students often write fascinating reactions to this exercise.

Learning Opportunity:
Self-Portrait

Objectives:
- To compare the artist's intent with the viewer's conceptions.
- To choose the objects and impressions that you want people to have about you after death.

Activity:
Assume that you are ordering a portrait to be painted of yourself because you will not live much longer. What would you put in this portrait to describe yourself and show your importance to future generations? Write a description of this work of art explaining your choice of pose, clothing, background, props, etc.

Notes to Teacher:
A helpful reference and class display might be a set of Rembrandt's self-portraits. These were done periodically as he got older.

If the students are willing to share what they have done, you might suggest the comparison of their intentions with the rest of the class's perceptions.

Selected Resources for Level IV ✌

Agee, James. *A Death in the Family.* New York: Avon, 1959.

Albee, Edward. *The Sandbox.* In *The Zoo Story, The Death of Bessie Smith, The Sandbox.* New York: Coward-McCann, 1960.

Anouilh, Jean. *Becket or The Honor of God.* New York: Coward-McCann, 1960.

Arundel, Honor. *The Blanket Word.* Nashville: Thomas Nelson, Inc., 1973.

Asinof, Eliot. *Craig and Joan: Two Lives for Peace.* New York, Viking Press, 1971.

Bach, Richard. *Jonathan Livingston Seagull.* New York: MacMillan Co., 1970.

Barnouw, Victor. *Dream of the Blue Heron.* New York: Delacorte Press, 1966.

Beckman, Gunnel. *Admission to the Feast.* New York: Rinehart & Winston, 1971.

Bedau, Hugo Adam, ed. *The Death Penalty in America.* Chicago: Aldine Publishing Co., 1964.

Bodsworth, Fred. *The Sparrow's Fall.* Garden City, N.Y.: Doubleday & Co., 1967.

Bolt, Robert. *A Man for All Seasons.* New York: Random House, 1960.

Bolton, Carole. *Reunion in December.* New York: William Morrow & Co., 1962.

Bronte, Emily. *Wuthering Heights.* London: Folio Society, 1964.

Brown, Raymond Lamont. *A Book of Epitaphs.* New York: Taplinger, 1967.

Buck, Pearl. *The Good Earth.* New York: John Day Co., 1931.

Caras, Roger. *Death as a Way of Life.* Boston: Little, Brown & Co., 1970.

Cleaver, Vera and Bill. *Where the Lilies Bloom.* Philadelphia: J.B. Lippincott, 1969.

Connolly, Edward. *Deer Run.* New York: Charles Scribner's Sons, 1971.

Considine, Millie and Pool, Ruth. *Wills: A Dead Giveaway.* Garden City, N.Y.: Doubleday & Co., 1974.

Crane, Stephen. *Red Badge of Courage.* New York: Random House, 1951.

Craven, Margaret. *I Heard the Owl Call My Name.* Garden City, N.Y.: Doubleday & Co., 1973.

deLeusse, Claude. *For Love of Anne.* New York: David McKay Co., 1973.

Donovan, John. *Wild in the World.* New York: Harper & Row, 1971.

Dooley, Thomas A. *Doctor Tom Dooley, My Story.* New York: Farrar, Straus & Co., 1960.

Drew, Elizabeth. *Poetry: A Modern Guide to Its Understanding and Enjoyment.* New York: Dell, orig., 1959.

Eckert, Allan W. *Incident at Hawk's Hill.* Boston: Little, Brown & Co., 1971.

Eliot, Thomas S. *Murder in the Cathedral.* London: Faber & Faber Ltd., 1935.

Elliott, Sumner Locke. *Going.* New York: Harper & Row, 1975.

Estes, Winston M. *Another Part of the House.* Philadelphia: J.B. Lippincott, 1970.

Euripedes. *The Trojan Women.* In *Three Greek Plays.* Translated by Edith Hamilton. New York: W. W. Norton & Co., 1937.

Fast, Howard. *The Hessian.* New York: William Morrow & Co., 1972.

Faulk, Ann Mari. *A Place of Her Own.* New York: Harcourt, Brace & World, Inc., 1962.

Faulkner, William. *As I Lay Dying.* New York: Harrison Smith & Robert Hass, 1930.

Gaines, Ernest J. *The Autobiography of Miss Jane Pittman.* New York: Dial Press, 1971.

Gallico, Paul. *The Snow Goose.* New York: A.A. Knopf, 1946.

Gann, Ernest K. *The High and the Mighty.* New York: Sloane, 1953.

Gardam, Jane. *The Summer After the Funeral.* New York: MacMillan Co., 1973.

Gillon, Edmond V. *Early New England Gravestone Rubbings.* New York: Dover Books, 1966.

Gloag, Julian. *Our Mother's House.* New York: Simon & Schuster, 1963.

Golding, William. *Lord of the Flies.* New York: Coward-McCann, 1962.

Graham, Gail. *Cross-Fire: A Vietnam Novel.* New York: Pantheon, 1972.

Gunther, John. *Death Be Not Proud.* New York: Harper & Brothers, 1949.

Guy, Rosa. *The Friends.* New York: Holt, Rinehart & Winston, 1973.

Hale, Edward Everett. *The Man Without a Country.* New York: Franklin Watts, 1960.

Hamilton, Edith. *Mythology.* Boston: Little, Brown & Co., 1942.

Harmer, Ruth Mulvey. *The High Cost of Dying.* New York: Collier Books, 1963.

Harris, Mark. *Bang the Drum Slowly.* New York: A.A. Knopf, 1956.

Hemingway, Ernest. *Across the River and Into the Trees.* New York: Charles Scribner's Sons, 1950.

————. "The Capital of the World;" "A Clean, Well-Lighted Place;" "The Short Happy Life of Francis Macomber;" "The Snows of Mt. Kilimanjaro;" and "Sordo's Stand" from *For Whom The Bell Tolls.* In *The Hemingway Reader.* New York: Charles Scribner's Sons, 1953.

————. *Death in the Afternoon.* New York: Charles Scribner's Sons, 1932.

————. *A Farewell to Arms.* New York: Charles Scribner's Sons, 1949.

————. *For Whom the Bell Tolls.* New York: Charles Scribner's Sons, 1940.

————. "Indian Camp;" "My Old Man." In *In Our Time.* New York: Charles Scribner's Sons, 1958.

————, ed. *Men at War: The Best War Stories of All Time.* New York: Croun Publishers, 1942.

————. *To Have and Have Not.* New York: Charles Scribner's Sons, 1937.

Hentoff, Nat. *I'm Really Dragged But Nothing Gets Me Down.* New York: Simon & Schuster, 1968.

Herbert, Frank. *Soul Catcher.* New York: G.P. Putnam's Sons, 1972.

Hersey, John. *Hiroshima.* New York: A.A. Knopf, 1946.

Hill, Susan. *In the Springtime of the Year.* New York: E.P. Dutton & Co., 1974.

Horwitz, Elinor Lander. *Capital Punishment, USA.* Philadelphia: J.B. Lippincott, 1973.

Hunter, Millie. *A Sound of Chariots*. New York: Harper & Row, 1972.

Hyde, Dayton O. *The Last Free Man*. New York: Dial Press, 1973.

Irion, Paul E. *The Funeral: Vestige or Value?* Nashville: Abingdon Press, 1966.

Johnson, A.E. *A Blues I Can Whistle*. New York: Scholastic Press, 1974.

Joyce, James. "The Dead;" "A Painful Case;" "The Sisters." In *Dubliners*. New York: Viking Press, 1962.

Kazantzakis, Nikos. *Zorba the Greek*. New York: Simon & Schuster, 1953.

Klein, Norma. *Sunshine*. New York: Avon Books, 1974.

Kotulak, Ronald. "Death definition meets test of life," *Chicago Tribune*, Feb. 2, 1975.

Lee, Mildred. *Fog*. New York: Seabury Press, 1972.

————. *The Rock and the Willow*. New York: Lothrop, Lee & Shephard, 1963.

Levy, Barbara. *Legacy of Death*. New York: Prentice-Hall, 1973.

Ludwig, Allan. *Graven Images*. Boston: Wesleyan Univ. Press, 1966.

Lund, Doris. *Eric*. Philadelphia: J.B. Lippincott, 1974.

McCullers, Carson. *The Heart Is a Lonely Hunter*. Boston: Houghton Mifflin Co., 1940.

Madison, Winifred. *Bird on the Wing*. Boston: Little, Brown & Co., 1974.

Mann, Thomas C. and Greene, Janet. *Over Their Dead Bodies: Yankee Epitaphs & History*. Brattleboro, Vt.: Stephen Greene Press, 1962.

Mason, Herbert M., Jr. *Death From the Sea*. New York: Dial Press, 1972.

Masters, Edgar Lee. *The New Spoon River*. New York: MacMillan Co., 1968.

————. *Spoon River Anthology*. New York: MacMillan Co., 1915.

Mathis, Sharon Bell. *Teacup Full of Roses*. New York: Viking Press, 1972.

Mazer, Norma Fox. *A Figure of Speech*. New York: Delacorte Press, 1973.

Miller, Arthur. *Death of a Salesman*. New York: Viking Press, 1949.

Mitchell, Margaret. *Gone With the Wind*. New York: MacMillan Co., 1936.

Mitford, Jessica. *The American Way of Death*. New York: Fawcett-World, 1969.

Mohr, Nicholasa. *Nilda*. New York: Harper & Row, 1973.

Morgan, Ernest. *A Manual of Death Education and Simple Burial*. Burnsville, N.C.: Celo Press, 1973.

Morris, Jean. *A Short Season*. New York: Rand-McNally, 1971.

Murphy, Shirley Rousseau. *Poor Jenny, Bright as a Penny*. New York: Viking Press, 1974.

Murray, Michele. *The Great Mother and Other Poems*. New York: Sheed & Ward, 1974.

Olsen, Tillie. "Tell Me a Riddle." In M. Foley and D. Burnett, eds. *The Best American Short Stories*. New York: Ballantine Books, 1962.

Peck, Robert Newton. *A Day No Pigs Would Die*. New York: A.A. Knopf, 1972.

Pine, Vanderlyn R. *Caretaker of the Dead: The American Funeral Director*. New York: Irving Publishers and John Wiley, Inc., 1975.

Plath, Sylvia. *Ariel*. New York: Harper & Row, 1966.

Platt, Kim. *Chloris and the Creeps*. Philadelphia: Chilton Book Co., 1973.

Puzo, Mario. *The Godfather*. New York: G.P. Putnam's Sons, 1969.

Rabin, Gil. *Changes*. New York: Harper & Row, 1973.

Read, Piers Paul. *Alive: The Store of the Andes Survivors*. New York: J.P. Lippincott Co., 1974.

Rhodin, Eric. *Good Greenwood*. Philadelphia: Westminster, 1971.

Rosenthal, Ted. *How Could I Not Be Among You*. New York: George Braziller, Inc., 1973.

Saint-Exupery, Antoine de. *The Little Prince*. New York: Reynal & Hitchcock, 1943.

Segal, Eric. *Love Story*. New York: Harper & Row, 1970.

Shaw, George Bernard. *Saint Joan*. In *Seven Plays*. New York: Dodd, Mead & Co., 1951.

Sherburne, Zoa. "From Mother . . . With Love." In *Stories from Seventeen*. Edited by Bryna Ivens. New York: J.B. Lippincott, 1955.

————. *Jennifer*. New York: William Morrow & Co., 1959.

Silverberg, Robert. *Born With the Dead*. New York: Random House, 1974.

————. *Recalled to Life*. Garden City, N.Y.: Doubleday & Co., 1972.

Spiegel, Fritz. *A Small Book of Grave Humour*. New York: Arco Publ. Co., 1973.

Stolz, Mary. *By The Highway Home*. New York: Harper & Row, 1971.

————. *The Edge of Next Year*. New York: Harper & Row, 1974.

Swados, Harvey. "The Tree of Life." *McCall's* (June, 1965), pp. 84-85.

Taylor, Theodore. *The Cay*. Garden City, N.Y.: Doubleday & Co., 1969.

Ter Haar, Jaap. *Boris*. New York: Delacourt Press, 1969.

Thomas, Dylan. *The Poems of Dylan Thomas*. Edited by Daniel Jones. New York: New Directions, 1971.

Trumbo, Dalton. *Johnny Got His Gun*. New York: Bantam Books, 1970.

Twain, Mark. *The Complete Short Stories of Mark Twain*. Garden City, N.Y.: Doubleday & Co., 1957.

————. *Letters From the Earth*. Greenwich, Conn.: Fawcett, 1968.

Updike, John. "My Uncle's Death." In *Assorted Prose*. New York, A.A. Knopf, 1965.

Uris, Leon M. *Exodus*. Garden City, N.Y.: Doubleday & Co., 1958.

Wallis, Charles L. *American Epitaphs, Grave and Humorous*. New York: Dover, 1973.

Watkin, Lawrence Edward. *On Borrowed Time*. New York: A.A. Knopf, 1937.

Waugh, Evelyn. *The Loved One*. Boston: Little, Brown & Co., 1948.

Wechsler, James A. *In A Darkness*. New York: Norton, 1972.

Wersba, Barbara. *Run Softly, Go Fast*. New York: Atheneum, 1972.

Wilder, Thorton. *The Bridge of San Luis Rey*. New York: A & C Boni, 1927.

Williams, Oscar, ed. *The Pocket Book of Modern Prose*. New York: Washington Square Press, 1958.

Williams, Tennessee. *The Rose Tatoo*. In *Three Plays*. New York: New Directions, 1964.

Windsor, Patricia. *The Summer Before*. New York: Harper & Row, 1973.

Woodford, Peggy. *Please Don't Go*. New York: E.P. Dutton & Co., 1972.

"You and Death Questionnaire." *Psychology Today*. 5 (August, 1970), pp. 67-72.

Zindel, Paul. *The Pigman*. New York: Harper & Row, 1968.

APPENDICES

Appendix A ✺
Guidelines From One Teacher's Unit
Introducing Death as a Literary Theme
By Ward Ghory

Teacher Goals:
- To help students become able to talk and think about death and life in their own experience.
- To help students realize how much they (and we and our culture) avoid or deny the realities of death.
- To help students see different literary ways of expressing grief, loss, and affirmation.

1) You as teacher might want to choose introductory texts, and begin with stories about characters at first unable to face death (like *Sixteen* by Jessamyn West or *Indian Camp* by Ernest Hemingway). In a number of suggestive ways, try to make the point clear that it's hard to talk about death and that most avoid doing so. Countless articles also make this point (E.K. Ross most effectively) and can be read. Before you get very far, it's crucial to establish the *need* for doing talking and reading about death, that it can be hard but it is worthwhile. You yourself should feel this if you're teaching the unit.

2) In general, allow students' personal experiences with death to surface spontaneously during this period, supporting them without probing too much. Avoid going around the room and confronting people, before they even have many ways of thinking about their experiences.

3) At first, read mostly *short* articles, stories or poems (elegies or odes even), encouraging as much discussion as possible. Movies (like *Chicamauga* or *My Old Man*), stories that aren't too heavy or strange (like *Garden Party* by Katherine Mansfield, or *My Old Man* by Ernest Hemingway) are appropriate. Resist overly formal analysis of stories and poems (you want to talk about death, not English jargon). Focus on characters and their attitudes — you'll find kids beginning to identify more easily this way. Look at form as a way of expressing and comprehending difficult emotion.

4) As a second stage in your planning, or when interest seems to emerge, suggest that the class and teacher talk more about deaths in their own experience. Here too is a place for some teacher structure: pass out a specific questionnaire (E.K. Ross questionnaire) for a quiet writing time, volunteer to talk first (honestly but easily) about a death in your family, start to provide models and tools for talking and thinking about death. Invite people to record dreams about death and look at these. Look at myths about life after death, and discuss the truths they express. Invite other outsiders, like a priest or doctor, to talk about death. Make sure to return to the students who have already volunteered some talk about their own experiences, and ask them questions in discussion, both to help them clarify their own experiences and to get discussion rolling. Begin to ask people who haven't volunteered what they think about a story or some other student's account, then ask them to compare it to their own experiences. Remember everyone sees death all around them but doesn't necessarily recognize it as such. Use newspapers and magazines, for example, to illustrate the numerous references to death all around us. We've all had experiences, and hold opinions; your goal as a teacher is to help bare the assumptions which underlie opinions, and lead your students to hold more mature reflections in their place.

5) As a third stage, now more extended, individual or student-centered projects are more likely to work. Prepare a bank of resource materials and possible topics. During discussion, listen for the key concerns different students express, and suggest they pursue these as individual or group topics. Longer readings, like novels, philosophy, sociology and psychology, are now appropriate. Much music expressing the emotions of death is also around. Especially encourage kids to articulate the way *they* see death in comparison to something they've read or heard. It's been my experience that students will find this difficult, unless they have been exposed to many points of view on death and had a lot of practice discussing the way other people relate to death.

6) For some students, a unit on death literature will be their initiation into a troubling, unknown realm. It may be others' first experience with using literature as a means to confront important themes in their own lives in an adult way. The teacher should help students use literature sometimes as a means to distance these

difficult realities, and other times as a means of personalizing others' experiences. This is the tightrope you may find yourself walking; between the extremes of uninspired, boring discussion about distant material, and intense group therapy about highly emotional concerns. Either extreme is unproductive. The balance your class finds depends in part on the amount of risk-taking you support and trust you inspire. When it's good, a unit on death-literature teaches as much about literature as it does about death; when it's bad, it's just another English class.

Appendix B ✿
Questions to be Explored
Through Fiction[13]

1. What is the range of possible human response to death of a family member? How does society or a given subculture sanction some reactions and determine the limits within which a family or a family member may express feelings?

2. What are the newer norms concerning the duration of mourning and its outward expression?

3. Does grief for loss of a role or of a relationship manifest itself differently than grief for loss of the given person?

4. Do all varieties of burial rites have the same effects on the feelings of the bereaved? On what basis can decisions be made concerning the open casket, cremation, ceremonial services, and the like? Whose body is it; what weight is to be given to the dying person's wishes if they conflict with those of other family members or with community standards? Why are there such conflicting feelings about the body of the deceased?

5. Is the bittersweet quality of the gathering of kin at a funeral typical or exceptional?

6. In what ways does bereavement precipitate out the confrontation with one's own mortality, with what possible consequences for the individual and the family?

7. What is the relationship between the duration and kind of dying (accident versus prolonged illness) and the mourning process?

8. What is the range of normality in the feelings of guilt and self accusation, in the expression of aggressive feelings, etc.?

9. What kinds of support can relatives, friends, neighbors, professionals (medical, religious, educational) provide that will

[13]Rose Somerville, *Introduction to Family Life and Sex Education* (New York: Prentice Hall, 1972), p. 352.

facilitate facing reality, completion of grief work, and reallocation of roles?

10. What is the relation of death and bereavement to the life philosophy, value system (individual, family, society) and coping mechanisms of each family member?

Knowledge of fiction that has a death or bereavement dimension can be gained by reading current book reviews or by consulting topical listings in catalogues such as *Short Story Index* and *Play Index*.

Appendix C
You and Death*

Note: In a few questions, you may find it necessary to circle more than one answer. If that is the case, please circle as many responses as you need to answer completely.

1. Who died in your first personal involvement with death?
   a. Grandparent or greatgrand-parent.
   b. Parent.
   c. Brother or sister.
   d. Other family member.
   e. Friend or acquaintance.
   f. Stranger.
   g. Public figure.
   h. Animal.

2. To the best of your memory, at what age were you first aware of death?
   a. Under three.
   b. Three to five.
   c. Five to ten.
   d. Ten or older.

3. When you were a child, how was death talked about in your family?
   a. Openly.
   b. With some sense of discomfort.
   c. Only when necessary and then with an attempt to exclude the children.
   d. As though it were a taboo subject.
   e. Never recall any discussion.

4. Which of the following best describes your childhood conceptions of death?
   a. Heaven-and-Hell concept.
   b. After-life.
   c. Death as sleep.
   d. Cessation of all physical and mental activity.
   e. Mysterious and unknowable.
   f. Something other than the above.
   g. No conception.
   h. Can't remember.

5. Which of the following most influenced your present attitudes toward death?
   a. Death of someone close.
   b. Specific reading.
   c. Religious upbringing.
   d. Introspection/meditation.
   e. Ritual (e.g. funerals).
   f. TV, radio, motion pictures.
   g. Longevity of my family.
   h. My health or physical condition.
   i. Other (specify):_____

6. Do you believe in life after death?
   a. Strongly believe in it.
   b. Tend to believe in it.
   c. Uncertain.
   d. Tend to doubt it.
   e. Convinced it does not exist.

NOTE TO TEACHER: Administering this questionnaire to your class (age 13+) and tabulating the results can lead to much productive discussion and many worthwhile projects dealing with death.

7. To what extent do you believe in reincarnation?
   a. Strongly believe in it.
   b. Tend to believe in it.
   c. Uncertain
   d. Tend to doubt it.
   e. Convinced it does not exist.

8. How often do you think about your own death?
   a. Very frequently (at least once a day).
   b. Frequently.
   c. Occasionally.
   d. Rarely (no more than once a year.
   e. Very rarely or never.

9. If you could choose, when would you die?
   a. In youth.'
   b. In the middle prime of life.
   c. Just after the prime of life.
   d. In old age.

10. Has there been a time in your life when you wanted to die?
    a. Yes, mainly because of great physical pain.
    b. Yes, mainly because of great emotional upset.
    c. Yes, mainly to escape an intolerable social or interpersonal situation.
    d. Yes, mainly because of great embarrassment.
    e. No.
    f. Other (specify): _____

11. What does death mean to you?
    a. The end; the final process of life.
    b. The beginning of a life after death; a transition, a new beginning.
    c. A joining of the spirit with a universal cosmic consciousness.
    d. A kind of endless sleep; rest and peace.
    e. Termination of life but with survival of the spirit.
    f. Don't know.
    g. Other (specify): _____

12. What aspect of your death is the most distasteful to you?
    a. I could no longer have any experiences.
    b. I am afraid of what might happen to my body after death.
    c. I am uncertain as to what might happen to me if there is a life after death.
    d. I could no longer provide for my dependents.
    e. It would cause grief to my relatives and friends.
    f. All my plans and projects would come to an end.
    g. The process of dying might be painful.
    h. Other (specify): _____

13. In your opinion, at what age are people most afraid of death?
    a. Up to 12 years.
    b. Thirteen to 19 years.
    c. Twenty to 29 years.
    d. Thirty to 39 years.
    e. Forty to 49 years.
    f. Fifty to 59 years.
    g. Sixty to 69 years.
    h. Seventy years and over.

14. To what extent do you believe that psychological factors can influence (or even cause) death?
    a. I firmly believe that they can.
    b. I tend to believe that they can.
    c. I am undecided or don't know.
    d. I doubt that they can.

15. When you think of your own death (or when circumstances make you realize your own mortality), how do you feel?
    a. Fearful.
    b. Discouraged.
    c. Depressed.
    d. Purposeless.
    e. Resolved, in relation to life.
    f. Pleasure, in being alive.
    g. Other (specify): _____

16. How often have you been in a situation in which you seriously thought you might die?
    a. Many times.
    b. Several times.
    c. Once or twice.
    d. Never.

17. To what extent are you interested in having your image survive after your own death through your children, books, good works, etc.?
    a. Very interested.
    b. Moderately interested.
    c. Somewhat interested.
    d. Not very interested.
    e. Totally interested.

18. For whom or what might you be willing to sacrifice your life?
    a. For a loved one.
    b. For an idea or a moral principle.
    c. In combat or a grave emergency.
    d. Not for any reason.
    e. Other (specify): _____
    _____

19. If you had a choice, what kind of death would you prefer?
    a. Tragic, violent death.
    b. Sudden but not violent death.
    c. Quiet, dignified death.
    d. Death in line of duty.
    e. Death after a great achievement.
    f. Suicide.
    g. Homicidal victim.
    h. There is no "appropriate" kind of death.
    i. Other (specify): _____
    _____

20. If it were possible, would you want to know the exact date on which you are going to die?
    a. No.
    b. Yes.
    c. Undecided.

21. If your physician knew that you had a terminal disease and a limited time to live, would you want him to tell you?
    a. Yes.
    b. No.
    c. It would depend on the circumstances.

22. If you were told that you had a terminal disease and a limited time to live, how would you want to spend your time until you died?
    a. I would make a marked change in my life-style.
    b. I would become more withdrawn; reading, comtemplating or praying.
    c. I would shift from my own needs to a concern for others.
    d. I would attempt to complete projects; tie up loose ends.
    e. I would make little or no change in my life-style.
    f. I would try to do one very important thing.
    g. I might consider suicide.
    h. I would do none of these.

23. How do you feel about having an autopsy done on your body?
    a. Approve.
    b. Don't care one way or other
    c. Disapprove.
    d. Strongly disapprove

24. Rank the following in terms of the role each has played in your present attitudes toward your own death.
    a. Changes in health conditions and mortality statistics
    b. Domestic violence.
    c. Existential philosophy.
    d. Family.
    e. Pollution of the environment.
    f. Possibility of nuclear war.
    g. Poverty.
    h. Religion.
    i. Television and movies.
    j. Wars.
    k. Other (specify): _____

25. How often have you fantas-
cized about committing
suicide?
   a. Very often.
   b. Only once or twice.
   c. Very rarely.
   d. Never.

26. Have you ever actually attempted suicide?
   a. Yes, with an actual very
high probability of death.
   b. Yes, with an actual moderate probability of death.
   c. Yes, with an actual low
probability of death.
   d. No.

27. To what extent do you believe
that suicide should be prevented?
   a. In every case.
   b. In all but a few cases.
   c. In some cases, yes; in others,
no.
   d. In no cases; if a person
wants to commit suicide
society has no right to stop
him.

28. What efforts do you believe
ought to be made to keep a seriously ill person alive?
   a. All possible effort; transplantation, kidney dialysis,
etc.
   b. Efforts that are reasonable
for that person's age, physical condition, mental condition, and pain.
   c. After reasonable care has
been given, a person ought
to be permitted to die a
natural death.
   d. A senile person should not
be kept alive by elaborate
artificial means.

29. How important do you believe
mourning and grief rituals
(such as wakes and funerals)
are for the survivors?
   a. Extremely important.
   b. Somewhat important.
   c. Undecided or don't know.
   d. Not very important.
   e. Not important at all.

30. If it were entirely up to you,
how would you like to have
your body disposed of after
your death?
   a. Burial.
   b. Cremation.
   c. Donation to medical school
or science.
   d. I am indifferent.
   e. Other (specify): _____
   _____

31. Would you be willing to donate
your heart or other body parts
for transplantation after you
die?
   a. Yes, to anyone.
   b. Yes, but only to a relative
or friend.
   c. I have a strong feeling
against it.
   d. No.

32. What kind of funeral would
you prefer?
   a. Formal, as large as possible.
   b. Small, relatives and close
friends only.
   c. Whatever my survivors want
   d. None.
   e. Other (specify):_____
   _____

33. How do you feel about "lying
in state" in an open casket at
your funeral?
   a. Approve.
   b. Don't care one way or the
other.
   c. Disapprove.
   d. Strongly disapprove.

34. What is your opinion about the
cost of funerals in the U.S.
today?
   a. Very much overpaid.
   b. No one has to pay for what
he doesn't want.
   c. In terms of costs and services rendered, prices are
not unreasonable.
   d. Other (specify): _____
   _____

35. In your opinion, what would be a reasonable price for a funeral?
  a. Under $300.
  b. From $300 to $600.
  c. From $600 to $900.
  d. From $900 to $1500.
  e. More than $1500.

36. What are your thoughts about leaving a will?
  a. I have already made one.
  b. I have not made a will, but intend to do so some day.
  c. I am uncertain or undecided.
  d. I probably won't make one.
  e. I definitely won't make one.

37. To what extent do you believe in life insurance to benefit your survivors?
  a. Strongly believe in it; have insurance.
  b. Tend to believe in it; have or plan to get insurance.
  c. Undecided.
  d. Tend to not believe in it.
  e. Definitely do not believe in it; do not have and do not plan to get insurance.

38. To what principally do you attribute the increase in concern with death in the U.S. in recent years?
  a. Wars.
  b. Domestic violence.
  c. Atomic and nuclear bombs.
  d. Pollution of environment.
  e. Existential philosophy.
  f. The drug culture.
  g. Television and movies.
  h. No change.
  i. Other (specify): _____
  _____

In order to evaluate this survey it is important to know a few things about the background of each person who responds. Please help by answering these questions.

39. What is your sex?
  a. Male.
  b. Female.

40. What is your age?
  a. Under 15.
  b. From 15 to 19.
  c. From 20 to 24.
  d. From 25 to 29.
  e. From 30 to 34.
  f. From 35 to 39.
  g. From 40 to 49.
  h. From 50 to 59.
  i. From 60 to 64.
  j. Over 64.

41. What is your religious background?
  a. Protestant.
  b. Roman Catholic.
  c. Jewish.
  d. Other.

42. What effect has this questionnaire had on you?
  a. It has made me somewhat anxious or upset.
  b. It has made me think about my own death.
  c. It has reminded me how fragile and precious life is.
  d. It has had no effect at all.
  e. Other effects (specify):
  _____
  _____
  _____

INDEX ✨